Kid's Box

New Generation

Caroline Nixon &
Michael Tomlinson

CAMBRIDGE

Student's Book
with eBook

American English

6

Language summary

	Key vocabulary	**Key language**	**Sounds and life skills**
⭐ **High technology** page 4	**Technology:** *app, blog, chat, competition, download, email, file, headphones, internet, laptop, microphone, online, smart speaker, smartphone, tablet, touch screen, turn on/off, TV show, upload, video games, Wi-Fi, win*	**Review of present tense** **Questions:** *Where is Robert? Why don't we write about video games? What do you think, Eva?*	**Stressed words** Social responsibilities
1 Beastly tales page 10	**Myths:** *beast, breathe, centaur, claws, dragon, eagle, feathers, fur, griffin, harpy (harpies), hero (heroes), horn, mermaid, myth, nest, phoenix, scales, siren, unicorn*	**Plans, intentions, and predictions with *going to*:** *Who are you going to see on the weekend? I'm going to see my cousins.* **Describing creatures:** *It has the body of a lizard. They have scales like a fish.*	**Word endings:** *-ing* Social responsibilities

	Key vocabulary	**Key language**	**Sounds and life skills**
2 Tomorrow's world page 18	**Space travel:** *air, astronaut, businessperson, Earth, engineer, float, Mars, moon, rocket, space, tourist, transportation, travel by (air/water)*	**Predictions with *will*:** *What transportation will we use in the future? I think we'll use carplanes.*	**Strong words** Creative thinking

	Key vocabulary	**Key language**	**Sounds and life skills**
3 The great outdoors page 28	**Exploration:** *adventure, backpack, break (arm/leg), camp, cave, east, expedition, explorer, flashlight, journey, land, north, rock, sleeping bag, south, tent, waterfall, west, wood*	**Past progressive and simple past:** *I was climbing up the mountain when it started to snow.* **Describing location:** *Oldbridge is east of the mountains.*	The /b/, /v/, and /w/ sounds Communication

	Key vocabulary	**Key language**	**Sounds and life skills**
4 Food, glorious food! page 36	**Food:** *butter, candy, chopsticks, cookie, dish, fruit, jam, paella, pan, pasta, peanuts, pizza, popcorn, sauce, snack, strawberry, sushi, vegetables*	**Countable and uncountable nouns:** *We don't have enough eggs. We have too much sugar and too many apples.*	**Strong words** Collaboration

High technology

? What technology do you use at home?

1 **What's the competition? Watch and check.**

2 ▶ **Watch again and number the sentences.**

1 We can meet at your house after. ☐
2 Hi, Eva. How are you? ☐ 1
3 We can write the best blog in the country. ☐
4 There's a new blog competition online. ☐
5 I have a message from Eva. ☐

STUDY

Where **is** he?
The children **have to** take their books to the library.
The winners **can** enter the international blog competition.
Sally **thinks** it sounds very exciting.

3 **Read and choose the right words.**

1 Robert **doesn't / don't** arrive early.
2 Where **has / is** Robert?
3 Sally and Robert **have / has** to take their books back to the library.
4 Robert **is / has** a message from Eva.
5 There **are / is** a prize for the best blog.

6 The winners can **enter / entering** the international blog competition next year.
7 Why **don't / doesn't** we do our first blog post on technology?
8 Sally thinks it **sound / sounds** very exciting.

4 **Ask and answer.**

1 What's the prize for the competition? Why do they want to win it?
2 Have you ever entered a big competition? What did you do?

Language: review of present tense

Can you remember the last lesson? Watch the language video.

 Read. Then listen and say "yes" or "no." Correct the wrong sentences.

National Blog Competition

Write a blog and help your school. It's open to all schools with students between the ages of 7 and 12. Students have to write a blog post every month. The blog post should be interesting and include text and pictures.

There are two important prizes. The best blog wins **new tablets** for everyone in your class. The winners can also enter the international blog competition next year.

 Read and answer.

 Sally: Hi, everyone. So, let's talk about our first blog post for the competition.

 Eva: Yes, great. What kind of technology should we write about?

 Robert: Why don't we write about video games?

 Eva: Good idea, Robert!

 Sally: Yes, I like that suggestion, but we should also write about other things. I'd like to write about online learning.

 Robert: OK. Should I write about video games? Then you can write about online learning, Sally. What do you think, Eva?

 Eva: That sounds good to me. Maybe I can write about technology at home?

 Sally: Yes, I love that idea. OK, everyone, no more chatting! Let's do it!

 Robert: See you at school tomorrow!

1 What are they chatting about?
2 What would Robert like to write about?
3 Does Eva like Robert's suggestion?
4 What does Sally think they should do?
5 Does Sally want to write about online shopping?
6 What's Eva going to write about?
7 Who wants to start now?
8 When are they going to meet again?

 Imagine you're going to write a blog post about your school. In groups, ask and answer.

1 What do you want to write about? Why?
2 Do your friends want to write about the same thing? Why or why not?

Useful language

Let's (talk about) …
What about …?
Why don't we (write about) …?
That sounds good to me.
Good idea.
I like that idea/suggestion, but we should …

 Write your blog post: "My school." Write 30–40 words.

Read the blog. What can technology give us? Find five things.

Kid's Box Reports

Technology is changing our lives a lot, so this is the topic of our first blog post of this year. People use technology every day when they work, study, or play.

Technology

We all use electronic devices like PCs (personal computers), **laptops**, **tablets**, and **smartphones** to connect with people and programs **online**. These days, most people have **Wi-Fi** at home, and we use different websites and apps when we go online.

Online learning

In some parts of the world, children don't go to school. They learn in an online classroom where they can communicate with their teachers and friends. Students have to turn on their cameras so that the teacher and class can see them, and the computer **screen** becomes their classroom and whiteboard. They use **headphones** or speakers to listen, and they talk into a **microphone**. When they have to do homework, they can send their teacher a **file** by **email** or they can **upload** it with an **app**.

Video games

Playing **video games** is one of the most popular hobbies for young people today. People can connect with a lot of players in different places all over the world to play and **chat** online.

E-sports is a kind of **competition** using video games for teams or single players. Millions of people can watch the competitors playing online, and it's very exciting. For some people, it is their job to play in online competitions, and they can earn money. We call these people gamers.

Technology at home

These days a lot of homes have a **smart speaker**. This device can answer questions about the weather, music, or TV shows, and, using Wi-Fi, people can connect it to other devices and ask it to do things. It can make a shopping list, **turn** the TV **on** or **off**, or control the temperature at home. Technology also helps in other ways. People can connect cameras in their house or yard, and watch their pets! Then, when they are not at home, they can see what their pets are doing and make sure they're safe.

 Read again and correct the sentences.

1 Laptops, tablets, and plants are electronic devices.
2 In an online classroom, students can communicate with teachers and insects.
3 When they have to do homework, they can send their teacher a postcard by email.
4 E-sports is a kind of meal using video games.
5 People can watch online competitions, and it's very boring.
6 People can't earn money by playing in video game competitions.
7 Smart speakers can make the beds.
8 With microphones, people can see the inside of their houses on their screens.

 Talk to a partner.

1 Which of these things do you use at home?
2 What kind of technology would you like to have? Why?

> I always send my homework to my teacher through our school app.

> I would like to have a smart speaker at home because I want to ask it a lot of questions.

1 Read and complete.

A smart speaker in the hall   And send pictures to our friends
~~Headphones, and big touch screens~~   Now turn off the Wi-Fi   We can use some apps as dictionaries

We have tablets in our backpacks,
An electronic smartboard on the wall.
There are laptops,
(1) Headphones, and big touch screens .
Hear the future call!

We have online learning.
We use smart technology
To find out what words mean.
(2) _____ .

Video things on our phones
(3) _____ .

We chat on our video games
And use programs to connect.

(4) _____ ,
And go out in the street.
You love chatting with all your friends
Every time you meet.

There are robots in our homes now,
(5) _____ .

It can answer everything we ask,
Hear the future call!

2 🎧 ▶ 3–4   Listen and check. Do karaoke.

3 Read and complete.

app   chat   ~~download~~   file   internet   likes   online   screen

Robert
Last week I got a cool new video game. The program was really big, so it took a long time to **(1)** download ,
but it's awesome. On Saturday, I'm going to play and **(2)** _____ online with friends from all over the world.

Eva
I enjoy taking pictures and making videos. I share them **(3)** _____ on a great **(4)** _____ called
CoolChat, which all of my friends use, too. I post my pictures there, and I sometimes get a lot of
(5) _____ ♥.

Sally
I love connecting to the **(6)** _____ to get information for my homework. I use my tablet, which has a
touch **(7)** _____ , so it's faster for me to work. I've finished my project on technology, and I've saved it in
a big **(8)** _____ . This evening I'm going to upload it for my teacher to read.

4 📝 Write about how you use technology. Write 30–40 words.

Sounds and life skills
Being a good school citizen

1 ▶ **Watch the video. How do they feel after they read about the competition?**

Pronunciation focus

2 🎧 5 **Listen and underline the stress in the words in bold. Write the words.**

EVA: ... let's write something for this **competition** and win those new **tablets** for our class.

ROBERT: Why don't we do our first blog on **technology**?

SALLY: Great idea, Robert! That sounds very **exciting**!

Oo	laptop keyboard _____
Ooo	internet microphone
oOo	computer _____
oOoo	_____
ooOo	_____

3 🎧 6 **Listen and complete. Practice with a partner.**

A: What _technology_ do you use every day?

B: I use the _____ for my homework.

A: Do you have a _____, a _____, or a _____?

B: I have a _____.

4 **Look and write more ideas.**

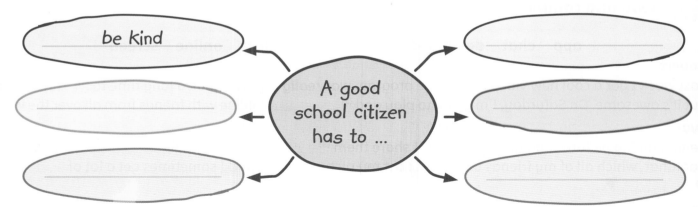

How to be a good school citizen

be kind

A good school citizen has to ...

5 **In pairs, make a poster about how to be a good school citizen.**

Diggory Bones

🎧 7 ▶

Sir Doug Bones! Nice to see you! So what time's Diggory's talk on the Sun Stone?

Um, hello, Iyam! Um, it's at half past two, after lunch.

CITY MUSEUM
CITY UNIVERSITY SCHOOL OF ARCHEOLOGY
AZTECHNOLOGY AND THE SUN STONE

You have one of the best rooms, Dad. I never have classes here.

Dr. DIGGORY BONES
AZTECHNOLOGY AND THE SUN STONE

One day, Emily, one day.

Um, Dad, is your talk ready? Is everything on your laptop?

Yes, yes, Emily. I'm turning it on now, and I have a copy on my flash drive, too.

Do you have the Sun Stone here in the college, Diggory?

Come on, Dad! It's ten after one. It's time for lunch.

Can I look under the cloth, Son? Can I see the calendar?

It's twenty-five to three.

AZTECHNOLOGY

Yes. I can use it to explain ancient math and technology.

No, Dad. It's a big surprise. You have to wait. OK. Let's go.

The Aztecs used one of the first math systems that the ancient mayas invented.

They used this math system to make their calendar, or Sun Stone.

What's this? I don't understand!

Clap! Clap! Clap!

What? Iyam Greedy!

Dad! It's the wrong photograph!

Press the button, Dad! Show the next photograph!

Surprise, Doctor Bones! We both know there are more secrets in the Sun Stone than math. You think you have it, but I have it now. If you want it, come and find me.

 What time's Diggory's talk? What should Diggory do to show the next photograph?

Story: unit language in context

9

1 Beastly tales

? What stories about animals do you know?

School play
King of the Beasts
★ ACTORS NEEDED ★
Auditions Wednesday 3:45 p.m.

1 ▶ What's Sally good at? Watch and check.

2 ▶ Watch again and answer the questions.

1 What time's the audition going to be? `Quarter to four.`
2 Who's going to go to the audition?
3 Which part is she going to do in the audition?
4 Who's going to be King of the Beasts?
5 Which part are they going to give Sally?
6 Are they going to write about the school play?

3 Read and match.

1 Who's going to
2 The audition
3 Sally's going to
4 Eva and Robert are
5 Sally isn't going
6 Eva and Robert aren't going
7 What are they going

a is going to be on Wednesday.
b to be in the play.
c go to the audition.
d to be the monkey.
e to write about?
f be in the play?
g going to watch her.

STUDY

I'm **going to go** to the audition.
We **aren't going to choose** you.
Are you **going to be** in the play?
What's Sally **going to be** in the play?

4 Ask and answer.

1 What did you think of Sally's acting?
2 Do you like acting? Would you like to be in a school play?

Language: plans, intentions, and predictions with *going to*

1 ▶ **Can you remember the last lesson? Watch the language video.**

2 **Choose the words from the box to complete the text.**

> bird ~~going~~ have island movie theater pets restaurant rocks see want

Helen and Robert are (1)_____going_____ to go to the (2)_____ tomorrow. They're going to (3)_____ a movie called *My Family and Other Animals*. The movie's from a book by Gerald Durrell, and it's about his life when he was ten years old. In the movie, the boy lives on an (4)_____ . He has some friends, but a lot of his friends are different (5)_____ . He has a (6)_____ named Ulysses, a turtle named Achilles, and a lot of spiders. Helen and Robert are going to have a great time because it's a very funny movie.

3 **Read again and answer. Check with a partner.**

1 Where are Helen and Robert going to go?
2 What are they going to see?
3 What's the movie about?
4 How old is Gerald in the book?
5 What pets does Gerald have?
6 Why are Helen and Robert going to enjoy the movie?

4 **Read and cross out the extra word.**

1 We're are going to go to the movie theater tomorrow.
2 We aren't going to see at *The Lion King*.
3 I'm going to visit to my grandmother on Sunday.
4 What are you to going to see?
5 Where do are you going to sit?
6 She isn't going to sing on tonight.

5 📝 **Write questions with "going to."**

1 Who / see / weekend?
2 What / do / Monday / after school?
3 play basketball / tomorrow afternoon?
4 Where / go / Friday / after school?
5 What / watch / TV / tomorrow?
6 When / do / your homework?

> 1 Who are you going to see on the weekend?

6 **Ask and answer.**

> Who are you going to see on the weekend?

> I'm going to see my cousins.

7 📝 **Write about what you're going to do next week. Write 30–40 words.**

1 **Read the blog. How many of the beasts are part bird?**

Kid's Box Reports

There are many ancient stories from different countries. Some are about **heroes** and strange and exciting **beasts** that aren't real. These stories are called **myths**.

Myths

Griffins have the head, wings, front legs, and **claws** of an **eagle** and the body and back legs of a lion. They make **nests** from gold.

A **unicorn** is a beautiful white horse with one long **horn** on its head. It has a goat's feet and beard, and a lion's tail.

A **dragon** is a beast that has the body of a lizard. Dragons don't have **fur** like a cat or **feathers** like a bird; they have **scales** like a fish. Some dragons have wings like a bat, and some can **breathe** fire.

Sirens and **harpies** are both part bird, part woman, but they're different. Sirens live near water. They sing beautifully, but they're dangerous because people sail their boats into rocks to listen to them. Harpies can't sing, but they can fly. They live in nests and steal food from people.

The **centaur** is part horse and part human. It has the head and top half of a man, and the body and legs of a horse.

Sometimes people think **mermaids** are the same as sirens, but mermaids are half woman, half fish. They have beautiful long hair, but they don't have legs. Instead they have a fish tail with scales.

2 **Read again and say "yes" or "no."**
Correct the wrong sentences.

1 Griffins make their nests from feathers.
2 A dragon has the body of a lizard.
3 A centaur has the legs of a goat.
4 A unicorn has two horns.
5 Sirens and harpies are part dragon and part woman.
6 Sirens steal people's food.
7 Harpies live in nests.
8 Mermaids have a big lizard tail.

3 **Talk to a partner.**

1 Which of these beasts do you think are the most interesting? Why?

> I think griffins are the most interesting because they make nests from gold.

2 Can you think of another beast from a story you know? What does it look like?

> A cyclops is a giant with one eye. It looks like a very big man!

1 🎧 **8** **Listen and choose the right words.**

1 The phoenix is a character in a **song** / **myth** / **game**.
2 The phoenix was a beautiful **bird** / **lion** / **horse**.
3 The phoenix lived for **five** / **fifty** / **five hundred** years.
4 The first people to believe in the phoenix were the **Egyptians** / **Romans** / **Greeks**.
5 The phoenix was born in a **pond** / **fire** / **tree**.

2 **Read and complete. Order the pictures.**

> clearer do Fleece Greece horse
> island sea sings song sports ~~told~~

Myths and legends, stories of old,
Beastly tales that people **(1)** ___told___ .
Adventures and monsters, strange animals, too,
Heroes who had great things to **(2)** _____ .

The Greeks are famous, not just for **(3)** _____ ,
But also for Jason and the Argonauts.
They wrote, in their mythology,
Of his adventures across the **(4)** _____ .

Jason's bad uncle made him look for the "fleece."
Special wool made of gold, so they tell us in
(5) _____ .

He had a smart teacher, like yours, of course!
His teacher was a centaur – half man, half
(6) _____ .

The teacher told him all about the dangerous siren
Who could break his boat on rocks around an
(7) _____ .
She's half woman, half bird, with feathers and wings.
She sounds really beautiful when she **(8)** _____ .

The Argonauts were sailing, and before too long,
They started to hear the siren's **(9)** _____ .
It sounded beautiful, but they didn't go nearer
'Cause Orpheus's music was louder and **(10)** _____ .

This is part of the myth from Ancient Greece
Of Jason and the Golden **(11)** _____ .

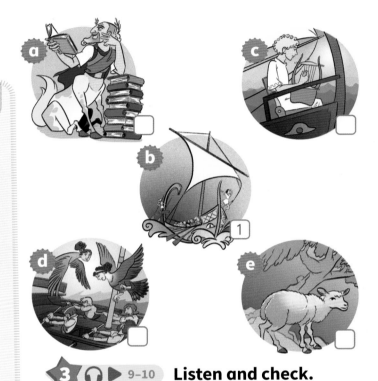

3 🎧 ▶ **9–10** **Listen and check. Do karaoke.**

4 **Invent an amazing mythical beast. Answer the questions.**

1 What are you going to call it?
  I'm going to call it a …
2 What's your beast going to look like?
  It's going to have a …'s head, …
3 What color's it going to be?
4 Is it going to have feathers, fur, or scales?
5 Is it going to have spots or stripes? What else is it going to have on its body?

5 **Ask and answer about your beast in pairs.**

6 📝 **Draw and write about your beast. Write 30–40 words.**

Sounds and life skills
Supporting your friends

1 ▶ **Watch the video. How does Sally feel before, during, and after the audition?**

Pronunciation focus

2 🎧 11 **Listen and write the word endings. Then practice with a partner.**

ROBERT: Well, I think you're good at sing_____!

SALLY: I'm go_____ to be a famous writer, start_____ with that blog competition! So, what are we going to write about this time?

ROBERT: Well, not *The K_____ of the Beasts!*

EVA: There are some older stories about other really excit_____ beasts.

3 🎧 12 **Listen and write. Say some more examples.**

I think you're good at _____ _____ .

Are you _____ to _____ in a competition?

4 🎧 13 **Listen and number. What other support can you give?**

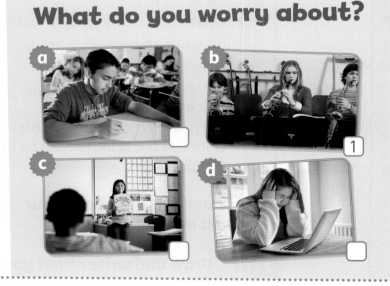

What do you worry about?

a

b   1

c

d

5 In pairs, do a role play.

Student A
You are worried about something. Tell your partner.

Student B
Listen to your partner. Give them some support.

Useful language

Good luck with …
Go for it!
You're good at it!
We're right here with you!

Diggory Bones

That beast Iyam Greedy has the Aztec calendar!

Who's Iyam Greedy, Grandpa?

He's the worst kind of pirate. He only looks for ancient treasure to get rich.

We don't have the calendar. How am I going to tell the museum in Mexico City?

Look, Dad! There's an envelope. It's for you!

What do these spots and stripes mean, Grandpa?

They look like that math system to me.

What? Let me see that!

Look! A spot means one, and a stripe means five ... hmmm.

Are you going to explain it to us, Son?

There are nine numbers. The first one's a spot with a stripe under it, so that's six.

Now I understand. It's 6, 1, 9, 3, 4, 2, 3, 9, 7. Does that mean anything?

It sounds like a phone number to me.

Well, let's try it. I'm going to put it on loudspeaker.

BEEP BEEP

Good work, Dr. Bones! I'm a snake, and I have feathers, but I can't fly. Are you going to fly?

Clap! Clap! Clap!

What does he mean?

He means Quetzalcóatl. He was part bird and part snake, and he was the most important god in Aztec mythology.

BING!

Plane tickets! Are you going to go to Mexico City, Son?

We are now. Come on, Emily! We have a job to do.

1 **Why is Iyam Greedy a bad pirate? Which god in Aztec mythology was part bird and part snake?**

Story: unit language in context   15

How have our toys and games changed?

1 🎧 **15** **Listen and read. Which toys or games do people still play with today?**

Fun and games in *ancient times*

Did you know that people in **ancient** times loved playing with toys and games just like we do today? In fact, many toys and games from the past are **similar to** modern ones. So how did people have fun a long time ago?

One of the oldest board games in the world is called senet, and it was very **popular** in ancient Egypt. Can you believe that people enjoyed playing it more than 4,000 years ago? Some people used a box with 30 squares and **counters** made of **bone**, but there were other ways to play it. Some people made their own game by drawing squares in the sand or on paper and using stones as counters, so it was a game for everyone.

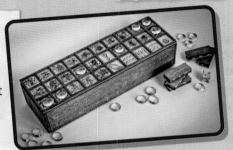

The ancient Greeks and Romans played games with **dice** made of bone, wood, or stone. The dice had six sides with spots on them to show the numbers, just like dice today. Some very early dice had only four **sides**, which were in the shape of a triangle. The oldest dice ever are about 5,000 years old!

People started playing with yo-yos more than 2,000 years ago. This painting shows a young Greek woman with a yo-yo. They were often made of wood, metal, or **terracotta**, and they had a string attached.

2 **Read again and complete the table.**

Toy/Game	Place	Time	Materials
(1) yo-yos	ancient Greece	2,000 years	(2) _____, metal, (3) _____, string
board game	(4) _____	(5) _____	bone, or sand, paper, and (6) _____
(7) _____	(8) _____ and ancient Rome	5,000 years	bone, wood, stone

3 **Which toys or games did you like when you were young? What entertainment is popular today?**

> I loved playing board games when I was young, but I like video games now.

> I think playing games on a smartphone is really popular today!

FIND OUT MORE
What are some other games people played in ancient times?

  History: toys and games | creative thinking

1 Read the review. How do you win this game?

| Blog | Game on! | Index |

START A GAME

GAME TIME

Clue ★ ★ ★ ★ ★

Clue is a classic board game that families have enjoyed since 1949! Everyone is a detective, and the winner is the player who solves the murder of Doctor Black. You need to use logic to discover the name of the murderer, the weapon they used, and the room where the murder happened.

The game has a board with a big house on it. Players use dice to move around, and when they are in a room, they can make guesses about the murderer, the weapon, and where the murder happened. You can use logic to figure out the correct answers. It's a game that usually takes between 10 and 60 minutes – not too long and not too short!

To play Clue, you need 3–6 players who are 8 years old or older. This makes it a perfect game for having fun with your family and friends.

I think every house should have Clue on their game shelf because it's a lot of fun and it helps you practice your problem-solving skills at the same time.

by Eliana

 2 Underline "who" and "that" in the review in Activity 1.

3 In pairs, discuss a game you know how to play. Answer these questions.

- How do you play the game?
- How long is it?
- How many players do you need?
- How old should they be?
- How do you win?
- Why do you like the game?

Learning to write:

who and that

We use *who* and *that* to connect two parts of a sentence.

Clue is a classic board game **that** families have enjoyed since 1949!

The winner is the player **who** solves the murder.

Ready to write:

Go to Workbook page 16.

Project

Make a board game.

2 Tomorrow's world

? How many types of transportation do you know

 What does the rocket do? Watch and check.

 Watch again and correct the sentences.

1 Eva's making a car.
2 Robert thinks we'll travel by water.
3 The rocket will swim.
4 The rocket will go to the stars.
5 Eva will get some pictures of rockets.
6 Their next blog post will be about the transportation of the past.

> Eva's making a rocket.

STUDY

We'll all **travel** by air.
Will it **fly**?
It **won't go** very far.

 Read and order the words.

1 the / hit / will / rocket / The / window.
2 fly? / Eva's / Will / rocket
3 stars. / won't / to / the / rocket / go / Eva's

4 will / hit? / rocket / the / What
5 another / won't / rocket / fly / backyard. / the / They /
6 transportation / be / of the / future. / will / Rockets / t

 Ask and answer.

1 Robert thinks rockets are the transportation of the future. Do you agree?
2 Do you enjoy doing science experiments? Describe your favorite one.

18 **Language:** predictions with *will*

1 **Can you remember the last lesson? Watch the language video.**

2 **Read and say the words.**

Transportation of the future!

It'll be a ⁽¹⁾ , not a ⁽²⁾ .

It'll pick up kids for school.

It'll stop for all of us.

Transportation of the future!

I'll have a computer on my ⁽³⁾ 🚲 .

It'll say, "Be careful!

⁽⁴⁾ 🚚 on right!"

So I'll ride it where I like!

Transportation of the future!

There won't be ⁽⁵⁾

or ⁽⁶⁾ 🚄 🚄 .

How'll we go on vacation?

We'll catch spaceships and spaceplanes.

Transportation of the future!

We'll have wings on all our

⁽⁷⁾  .

Where do you think we'll go?

We'll fly up to the stars.

Transportation of the future!

We'll take a ⁽⁸⁾ to the moon.

When'll we leave planet Earth?

We'll leave here very soon!

3 🎧 ▶ 16–17 **Listen and check. Do karaoke.**

4 **Read and answer.** **2**

In the future, we won't drive on roads and highways. We'll use carplanes, which will fly three meters above the ground. They will carry six people. They won't have a pilot because a computer will fly them. There'll be a small round table and six armchairs with cushions inside, like a small living room. There'll be a robot waiter to give us food and drinks. We'll chat on the internet and watch our favorite videos on big computer screens.

There won't be any normal doors. The sides of the carplane will open by moving slowly down under the floor of the car. There won't be any maps, and we'll never get lost because carplanes will always know where to go.

1 What transportation will we use in the future?
2 How high will carplanes fly?
3 Why won't a carplane have a pilot?
4 What kind of chairs will there be inside?
5 What will the inside of a carplane look like?
6 Why will it be easy to travel without maps?

5 **Do you think these things will happen? Why or why not?**

In 2075 …

1 people will eat different food.
2 children won't need to go to school.
3 everyone will have a robot that looks like a person.
4 no one will drive cars or trains.
5 there won't be any smartphones.
6 people will keep their memories on a microchip in their head.
7 waiters in restaurants will be robots.
8 people will wear different clothes.

6 **Work in pairs. Talk about what life will be like in 2075.**

I think we'll eat different food.

Really? What kind of food do you think we'll eat?

7 📝 **Write about your city in 2075. Write 30–40 words.**

1 **Read the blog. What are the three different kinds of space tourists?**

ALL BLOGS   MY BLOG   NEW POST

Kid's Box Reports

Our next blog post is about space travel. The first man walked on the moon in 1968, but now engineers are designing rockets which will send astronauts to Mars.

Space travel

The most important space agencies in the world are NASA (in the U.S.A.), ESA (in Europe), and the Russian, Chinese, and Indian space programs. They build rockets and teach astronauts how to fly them. Rockets take a long time to build and cost a lot of money, so they're too expensive to use as normal transportation.

A new space program called Artemis is planning different kinds of missions that will help us explore space. Some of these missions will take people to the moon and to Mars. The astronauts on these missions will live on a giant space station called the Gateway, which will stay in space for more than ten years. On the Gateway, astronauts will make and recycle air and water so they can live in space for a long time.

Some businessmen are helping space agencies to build better and cheaper rockets because they are interested in space travel and they want to send tourists into space and to the moon. Space tourists are people who are not astronauts, but want to visit space. It's a very expensive adventure! In 2021, a Japanese billionaire businessman paid nearly $35 million to stay on the International Space Station for 12 days. He is called an "orbital space tourist"

because he traveled around the Earth. "Sub-orbital space tourists" can go to see Earth from above, but they don't orbit it. They fly higher than 100 km above Earth which is where space starts, and for about five minutes they float inside the spaceship. One day, "lunar tourists" will travel outside Earth's orbit. They travel to the moon, and in the future they'll be able to go to Mars, too.

2 **Read again and answer.**

1 Where are the five most important space agencies?
2 Name two problems with rockets.
3 Who flies rockets?
4 What will astronauts do when they live on the Gateway?

5 What are businessmen helping space agencies to do?
6 How much did it cost the businessman to travel around Earth?
7 How far from Earth is space?
8 Where will space tourists travel in the future?

3 **Talk to a partner.**

1 Do you think you'll ever travel to the moon? Why or why not?

2 Would you like to go to Mars? Why or why not?

> No, I don't. Because I don't have a lot of money!

> I would like to go to Mars because I love adventures.

1 Look at the pictures. Read and order the words.

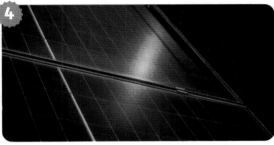

1 and make / Engineers / spaceships. / will design
2 in space stations / will stay / Space tourists / for their vacations.
3 on Mars but / will work / not on the sun. / Robots
4 Rockets and / solar energy. / will use / other transportation

2 🎧 18 Listen and answer. What is the man designing?

3 🎧 19 Listen again and write.

Name: (1) _____Robert_____
Last name: (2) _____
Dream job: (3) _____
Age next birthday: (4) _____
Present job: (5) _____
Rocket name: (6) _____

4 📝 Write questions with "will."

1 When / go / space?
2 What kind of clothes / wear / space?
3 What kind of food / eat / space?
4 What / take / pictures of?
5 Who / go with?
6 What / take / with you?

1 When will you go to space?

5 Imagine you are an astronaut. Ask and answer.

When will you go to space?   Well, I think I'll go next year.

Sounds and life skills
Choosing a point of view

1 ▶ Watch the video. What do Robert and Sally think about the rocket?

Pronunciation focus

2 🎧 20 Listen and underline the strong words. Then practice with a partner.

ROBERT: Soon there won't be any buses or cars – we'll all travel by air.

SALLY: Or we'll walk. We'll still have legs!

ROBERT: Will it fly?

3 🎧 21 Listen and complete. Practice with a partner.

A: In the future, we'll _____ .

B: And we won't _____ .

A: Will we _____ ?

B: I'm not sure.

4 📝 In pairs, think of and write more examples.

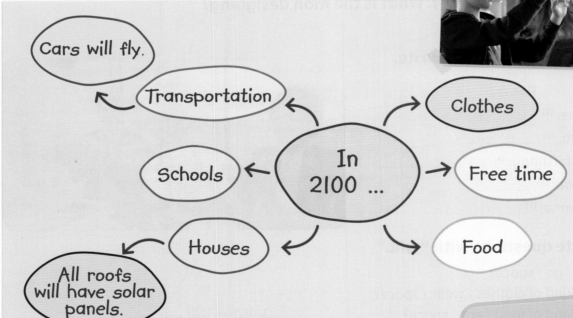

Cars will fly.

Transportation

Clothes

Schools

In 2100 ...

Free time

Houses

Food

All roofs will have solar panels.

5 In a group, discuss your predictions. Do you agree?

I agree, I think we will …

I don't agree. We won't … because …

Useful language

In the future, I think we'll …
We won't …
I agree / I don't agree because …

This is the last call for flight MYTC 155 to Mexico City. Will passengers please go quickly to Gate 6.

Come on, Emily. That's our plane. We'll have to run.

Why did Iyam Greedy send us tickets to Mexico City?

It was the most important Aztec city, and there are legends about Aztec gold.

The sun, moon, and stars were very important to both the Aztecs and the Mayas.

Like us, they used them to measure time, but they had two different calendars.

One with months and seasons for their work, and one for their mythology.

Hmm, they watched this big group of stars very carefully.

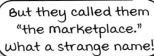

The Pleiades. The Aztec new year started when they could see these stars in the early morning, before the sun.

But they called them "the marketplace." What a strange name!

June 21st will be the longest day of the year. That was also very important in Aztec mythology.

It's June 18th, now! Do you think the secret of the Aztec gold's in their calendar, Dad?

I don't know, but you should try to sleep now.

Yes, I will. It'll take about ten hours to get there.

We won't stay in Mexico City tonight, Emily. We have to get to Teotihuacán before Greedy.

What's at Teoti ... what's there, Dad?

I don't know, but soon it's the longest day of the year.

 What did the Aztecs and the Mayas use to measure time? When did the Aztec new year start?

Story: unit language in context   23

What can robots do for us?

LIFE WITH ROBOTS

Did you know that a robot called Raptor can run 46 km an hour? That's much faster than the fastest human on Earth! Humans make robots with computer technology, and they help us do different kinds of jobs.

In 1961, a factory in the U.S.A. used the world's first industrial robot. It was a robot arm that could pick up hot metal to make cars, which is a dangerous job that's difficult for humans to do. Robots work faster than people, too, so they help factories **produce** more.

In hospitals, medical robots help doctors do important jobs. For example, special machines can **perform surgery** if the doctor's hand is too large. And doctors can even do surgery from a distance. They use computers to control robots that perform **remote surgery** on people who are in a different hospital.

At home, a domestic robot makes life easier for humans. These robots can clean, take care of your pets, or keep your home safe thanks to a **built-in alarm**. They can even **entertain** you! Some **robot devices** can answer questions, play your favorite music, and search the internet for you!

Humans have used space robots since the 1950s. The first space robot to go all the way t Mars was called Viking. Viking's job was to take pictures of Mars to help us learn more about the planet. Since then, five different **robot vehicles** called rovers, have traveled to Mars, too. These robots do a lot of **research** to find out if humans will be able to visit Mars in the future.

2 Read again and answer.

1 Which robot would you choose to do important research for humans?   *A space robot.*
2 Which robot would you choose to help with housework?
3 Which robot would you choose to do surgery on someone?
4 Which robot would you choose to do jobs that aren't safe for humans?
5 Which robot would you choose to take pictures of another planet?

3 Have you ever used a robot device? What can you use it for?

> We have a robot device at home. I can talk to it and ask it questions.

> What does it say?

> It tells me the time and what the weather's like.

FIND OUT MORE
The RoboBee is one of the smallest robots in the world! What does it look like?

1 Read the instructions. What kind of robot is it? Write.

DID YOU KNOW...?

Robots can travel very far from home! It took the spacecraft carrying the Perseverance rover seven months to reach Mars. It had to travel about 480 million km to get there!

How to make a

_____ robot

Materials

You will need paper, pencils, scissors, and craft materials.

Instructions

1 Plan your robot. Think about your robot and answer these questions:
- What will it do?
- What will it look like?
- How far will it travel?
- How will it move in space? (Rockets? Solar power?)
- What other special things will it have? Will it have wheels, arms, or cameras to take pictures?

2 Draw a picture of your robot and label all of the parts.

3 Build your robot. Use any materials you can find. If something doesn't work, don't worry. Try a different way.

4 Test your robot. It will need to land on a planet, so it will need to be strong. Shake it and check it doesn't break.

5 Give your robot an exciting name. Mars rovers in the past were called Perseverance, Spirit, and Opportunity!

2 Underline the instruction verbs in the instructions in Activity 1.

3 In pairs, discuss ideas for a new robot. Make notes in your notebook.

Learning to write:

Instructions

We use a verb, or *Don't* + verb, to give instructions.

Plan your robot.

If something doesn't work, **don't worry**.

what it looks like:

_____
_____
_____

My Robot

how it works:

_____
_____

what it does:

_____
_____

Ready to write:

Go to Workbook page 24.

Project

Follow the instructions and make a robot.

Review Units 1 and 2

1 **Read the text. Choose the right words and write them on the lines.**

The moon is ⁽¹⁾ ___Earth's___ only natural satellite. That means that the moon ⁽²⁾ _____ around the Earth once every 27 days. It is ⁽³⁾ _____ than Earth, and ⁽⁴⁾ _____ diameter is 3,474 km.

The first visit to the moon was ⁽⁵⁾ _____ July 20, 1969, ⁽⁶⁾ _____ Neil Armstrong, an American astronaut, ⁽⁷⁾ _____ the first man to walk on the moon. The U.S.A. sent rockets with astronauts to the moon over three years, but they stopped in 1972 because it was very expensive. Now different space agencies ⁽⁸⁾ _____ they will send astronauts to the moon again. The American, the Russian, the Chinese, the Indian, and the European space agencies all have plans for missions to the moon. NASA ⁽⁹⁾ _____ to build a camp at one of the lunar poles. It is doing tests in Antarctica to see how well it ⁽¹⁰⁾ _____ . It wants astronauts to visit the moon again so it can plan to fly to Mars!

1	Earth	Earth's	Earth is
2	goes	went	go
3	more	small	smaller
4	it's	its	her
5	in	for	on
6	when	who	where
7	is	was	were
8	say	says	saying
9	can	will	wants
10	works	work	working

2 🎧 24 **Listen and color and write. There is one example.**

THE PLANETS AND

3 **Play the game.**

Rocket launch
Instructions:

- English is the international language of space. USE it or LOSE a turn!
- Throw a dice and move around the board. First, collect a rocket, fuel, and food on Earth.
- When you have all three, continue to the LAUNCH square and fly to the moon.
- When you reach the LAUNCH square, fly to Mars. How will you help the planet?
- Read and follow all the instructions as you move around the board. Race to the END!

3 The great outdoors

? What activities do you like doing in the great outdoors?

1 ▶ **Where did Robert break his arm? Watch and check.**

2 ▶ **Watch again and say "yes" or "no." Correct the wrong sentences.**

1 Robert broke his arm last Friday.
2 Robert was walking when he fell.
3 Robert was jumping when he broke his arm.
4 Robert put his foot in a hole when he was crossing the bridge.
5 Robert was taking his boot off when he fell over.

> No. Robert broke his arm last Saturday.

STUDY

I **was jumping** when I **fell**.
Were you **playing** when you **broke** your arm?
No, I **wasn't playing**.

3 **Read and choose the right words.**

1 Robert and his dad **was / were** climbing a hill.
2 Robert **was / wasn't** playing when he fell over.
3 They were **walking / walks** across a bridge when Robert put his foot in a hole.
4 They **wasn't / weren't** having a picnic in the woods.
5 Robert didn't break his arm when he **is / was** crossing the bridge.
6 He was **taking / took** his boot off when he fell over.

4 **Ask and answer.**

1 What did you think of Robert's big adventure?
2 Have you or one of your friends ever broken a bone? What happened?

Language: past progressive and simple past

1 ▶ **Can you remember the last lesson? Watch the language video.**

2 **Read and complete.**

> And I had to jump out   Go down a waterfall   It didn't make a sound
> ~~There was nowhere else to go~~   Was racing after me

I was climbing up the mountain
When it started to snow.
I hid in a cave.
(1) _There was nowhere else to go_ .
What an adventure!

I was swimming down a river
When I thought I saw a tree.
A big crocodile
(2) _____ .
What an adventure!

I was flying over an island.
I was looking all around
When my plane coughed and stopped,
(3) _____ .
What an adventure!

I was sailing on a river,
Enjoying it all.
Then I saw a boat in front of me
(4) _____
What an adventure!

I was camping in the jungle.
I was sleeping on the ground
When suddenly I felt a snake.
(5) _____ .
What an adventure! What an adventure!

3 🎧▶ 25–26 **Listen and check. Do karaoke.**

4 **In groups, say what happened next.**

5 **Play the game.**

1 Listen to your teacher. Write your answer at the top of a piece of paper.
2 Fold the paper and pass it to the classmate on your left.
3 You can read the story when you answer the last question.

6 📝 **Write the story from the game.**

My name's Diggory Bones.
I was on a space rocket at 4 o'clock last Saturday afternoon.
I was wearing a swimsuit and sunglasses.

1 **Read the blog. Which journey do you think is the most exciting? Why?**

ALL BLOGS   MY BLOG   NEW POST

Kid's Box Reports

We always want to find out more about the planet where we live. **Explorers** travel to new places to learn new things.

Exploration

Marco Polo

Marco Polo was not the first European to travel **east** to China, but he is the most famous because of his books.

A lot of people have read them, including the explorer Christopher Columbus. Marco left Italy in 1271 and returned 24 years later. When he went to China, he traveled mostly over **land**, but when he came back to Europe, he traveled mostly by water. He brought back the idea of paper money, which people later copied.

Zara Rutherford

In 2021, Zara Rutherford became the youngest female pilot to fly around the world by herself. She began her **journey** in Belgium and flew **west**, and she stopped in 31 countries on five different continents! It took her five months to travel more than 50,000 km in a special plane called an ultralight. This is a plane so small a person can push it. Because her plane was so small, she couldn't carry a lot of things with her, but she had a **backpack**, a **sleeping bag**, and a **flashlight** to see in the dark.

Felicity Aston

Felicity Aston is another famous explorer. She began her **adventures** in 2000 when she traveled to Antarctica for the first time. She has been on **expeditions** all around the world, but especially to the **North** and **South** Poles. She skied across Antarctica alone in 2012. It took her 59 days to cover 1,744 km, so she had to **camp** in a **tent** every night. She was the first woman to do it. She has written books about her adventures and has won a lot of prizes for her work.

2 **Read again and correct the sentences.**

1 Marco Polo traveled east to Australia.
2 Marco Polo wrote a newspaper about his trip.
3 Zara Rutherford flew around the world with her parents.
4 A backpack is a bag you can sleep in.
5 An ultralight is one of the biggest planes in the world.
6 Felicity Aston began her adventures in 2021.
7 Felicity Aston was the first woman to snowboard across Antarctica.
8 Felicity Aston has designed video games about her adventures.

3 **Talk to a partner.**

1 Which of these explorers do you think had the most difficult adventure? Why?

> I think Felicity Aston had the most difficult adventure because she skied across Antarctica alone!

2 Where would you like to explore? Why?

> I would like to explore China because I have never been there and I like Chinese food.

Read and match. Say the word and the letter.

 a  b  c  d  e

1 It's something you use to see in the dark.
2 It's a big bag that you carry on your back.
3 It's like a small house. You use it when you go camping.
4 It's something that you sleep in.
5 It's someone who travels to a new place to learn about it.

flashlight – d

 Look at the map and say "yes" or "no." Correct the wrong sentences.

1 Clidditch is north of Ness Lake.
2 Alchester is south of the Deep Sea.
3 Mainwitch is east of the Deep Sea.
4 Hamptonville is north of Deer Wood.
5 Clidditch is south of Littleton.
6 Oldbridge is east of the mountains.
7 The mountains are south of Mainwitch.
8 Littleton is west of Mainwitch.

3 Play the game.

It's south of Clidditch and west of Oldbridge.

Is it Ness Lake?

Yes!

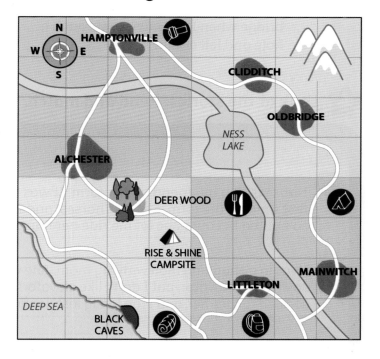

4 🎧 27 **Listen. What camping things do you pick up? Where are you?**

 Write about an adventure. Use the map and as many words in the box as you can.

beach   bridge   cave
grass   hill   lake
mountain   plan
river   rock   waterfall

One day I was walking near the Black Caves
by myself when ...

Sounds and life skills
Imagining possibilities

1 ▶ **Watch the video. How did Robert break his arm?**

Pronunciation focus

2 🎧 28 **Listen and read. Underline the sounds /b/, /v/, or /w/.**

SALLY: So, were you playing when you broke your arm?

ROBERT: No, I wasn't playing, Sally, and that wasn't when I broke my arm. We were in the woods, and we had to cross a very fast river. We were walking across the bridge when I put my foot through a hole and fell again.

3 🎧 29 **Listen and write. Practice with a partner.**

We were walking	on a _____	when I broke my arm.
	over a very fast _____	
	up a big _____	
	near a beautiful _____	

4 **Look at the stories. Read and match.**

What an adventure!

1 I was visiting my friend on her farm. It was my first time on the farm. She has horses, and I was so excited because she let me ride her horse!

a I was running down so fast that I couldn't stop! I fell and broke my arm! ☐

2 I was in a shopping mall with my mom. She went down in an elevator, but I don't like elevators, so I decided to race her, and I ran really fast down the stairs.

b I was climbing up to get it when I fell and, yes, I broke my arm! ☐

3 It was a very windy day, so I was flying my kite in the park. My kite was flying really high when it flew into a tall tree.

c It was walking quietly when suddenly it started to go fast. I fell off and broke my arm. ☐

5 **In pairs, imagine you are Robert and tell your story. Choose some of these places.**

How did you break your arm?

(at a museum) (on a camping trip) (at the amusement park)

(in the park) (in the classroom) (on a farm) (in the mountains)

Useful language

I was (walking) when I …
We were (playing) in the park when I …

Diggory Bones

🎧 30 ▶

I thought Mexico City was the most important Aztec city, Dad.

That's what Greedy wants us to believe.

The Aztecs built and lived in Tenochtitlán, which is now called Mexico City, but Teotihuacán, is much older.

Greedy said, "I'm a snake, and I have feathers, but I can't fly."

Of course! The Temple of Quetzalcóatl. It's near the pyramids in the ancient city of Teotihuacán!

We're only 40 km northeast of Mexico City. If I'm wrong, we can easily go back.

I don't think you're wrong ...

Good morning. I was sitting on the plane next to you yesterday. My name's Tricker, Richard Tricker.

Good morning, mr. Tricker. Will you join us for breakfast?

You were talking about the pyramids. I often take tourists there.

We're not ...

That's good. Will you take us there today?

Good job, Diggory! Now we're going on an adventure, and you'll need your backpacks. Here they are.

Quetzalcóatl, the Aztec god of the world. The snake shows Earth and plants, and feathers show the air and sky.

Let's go over there now.

This long street goes from north to south. It joins the Pyramid of the Sun and the Pyramid of the moon.

The Pyramid of the Sun is the highest in the world, and its west face is in line with the Pleiades.

Clap! Clap! Clap!

Hello, lyam. I was expecting to meet you here.

PLONK!

1 **What was the old name for Mexico City? Which pyramid is the highest in the world?**

Story: unit language in context

33

What can we see in our world?

1 🎧 31 **Listen and read. Write the headings.**

Cold mountains   How are mountains formed?   The highest and the longest
The young and the old   We are mountaineers!   ~~What is a mountain?~~

1 What is a mountain?

A mountain is a **landform** that stands **high above** the land around it. There are mountains all over the world. Scientists have even found huge mountains under the ocean. We call a lot of mountains standing together a **mountain range**.

2 _____

Mountains take millions of years to form. When two **plates** in the **Earth's crust** push together over a very long time, all the rocks slowly build up and up, until they make a mountain!

crust

3 _____

The Himalayas started **forming** 40–50 million years ago in Asia. The world's highest mountain, Mount Everest, is in the Himalayas. Everest is still growing and gets taller every year! The Himalayas are about 2,600 km long, but the Andes in South America are 7,000 km long, and they're the longest mountain range in the world.

4 _____

The Himalayas are millions of years old, but they are the youngest mountains on Earth. The Makhonjwa Mountains in South Africa formed about 3.6 billion years ago, and they are older than any other mountain range.

5 _____

Mountains are cold because they're high. Even mountains in hot countries can have snow on top! But the coldest mountain of all is Denali in Alaska. It's the highest **peak** in North America.

6 _____

A lot of people love climbing mountains, and about 4,000 people have already climbed Mount Everest. But other mountains are much harder to climb. K2, also in the Himalayas, is one of the most dangerous mountains to climb because of its shape.

 2 **Read again and complete the table.**

Mountain Range	Continent	Length	Age	Highest Peak
The Himalayas	1 _____	2 _____	3 _____	4 _____
The Andes	5 _____	6 _____	over 50 million years	Mount Aconcagua

 3 **Which mountain range would you like to visit? Why?**

I'd like to visit the Himalayas because I'd like to see Mount Everest.

FIND OUT MORE
What's the name of the highest mountain in your country?

Geography: mountains | 🛡 critical thinking

1 **Read the profile. Why does the writer admire Malavath Poorna?**

DID YOU KNOW…?
On Mars, there is a mountain called Olympus Mons that is two and a half times higher than Mount Everest!

3

Malavath Poorna

Malavath Poorna is an Indian mountaineer. I admire her because she's the youngest girl in the world to climb Mount Everest. She was only 13 years old when she reached the top of the world's highest mountain.

She was born in a small Indian village, far from the Himalayas. She worked hard at school and liked doing sports. One day, she was doing track and field when a teacher saw her talent. He chose her for an Everest expedition. It was a challenge, but she trained for three months to get ready to climb the mountain.

I think Malavath Poorna is very brave to do something so difficult. But she said she was never scared and wanted to make her family proud.

She likes climbing mountains on other continents, too, for example Mount Kilimanjaro, which is Africa's highest mountain, and Mount Aconcagua in South America.

I really like hiking, so I'd also like to climb a mountain one day. I think that to achieve something special you need to be strong and work very hard.

By Lakshay

2 **Underline examples of "like" + -ing and "would like to" + infinitive in the profile in Activity 1.**

3 **In pairs, discuss someone you admire. Make notes in your notebook.**

Name:

Date of birth:

Country:

Likes:

Achievement:

Why I admire them:

Learning to write:

like + –ing and *would like to + infinitive*

We use *like + -ing* to talk about what we enjoy.

We use *would like* + infinitive to talk about what we want to do.

I **like climbing**. One day, I**'d like to climb** Ben Nevis, the highest mountain in the U.K.

Ready to write:

Go to Workbook page 34.

Project

Make a fact file about a landform.

4 Food, glorious food!

? How many different dishes can you cook?

1 **What four ingredients do you need to make tarte Tatin? Watch and check.**

2 **Watch again and number the sentences.**

1 We have three kilos of sugar, too. We have too much! ☐
2 We don't have enough eggs, either. ☐
3 Do we have enough flour? ☐
4 We have too much sugar and too many apples. ☐
5 That's a kind of apple pie in French. ☐1☐
6 I think we have too many apples. ☐

STUDY

You'll need **enough** apples to cover the base.
We **don't** have **enough** eggs.
Do we have **enough** flour?
We have **too many** apples.
We have **too much** sugar.

3 **Read and order the words.**

1 has / apples. / a / big bag / Eva / of
2 many / They / apples. / too / have
3 a / They / of flour. / little bit / have
4 don't have / flour. / They / enough
5 one / only / have / They / egg.
6 flour or / enough / don't have / They / eggs.

4 **Ask and answer.**

1 What mistakes did the children make? Why did it happen?
2 Are you good at baking? What can you bake?

Can you remember the last lesson? Watch the language video.

 32 Listen and mark (✓) the box.

1 What does Michael want in his coffee?

2 What did Paul put on the table?

3 What does Robert want on his pasta?

4 What did Mary put on the table?

5 How many pizzas did Emma cook?

3 **Look and correct the sentences.** 4

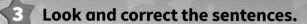   

1 There are too many knives.
2 There aren't enough spoons.
3 There are too many pizzas.
4 There isn't enough lemonade.
5 There are too many peas.
6 There isn't enough strawberry ice cream.

4 **In pairs, ask and answer ten questions with these words. Write your partner's answers.**

candy cheese chocolate eggs fish
fries fruit meat pasta pizza salad
soup strawberries vegetables

How often do you eat candy?

Twice a day. How often do you eat fish?

Three times a week.

5 **Talk to your partner.**

I think I eat too many fries. What do you think?

I think you eat too many fries too, and I …

6 **With your partner, tell another pair.**

We think we don't eat enough fruit because we only eat fruit once a day, and …

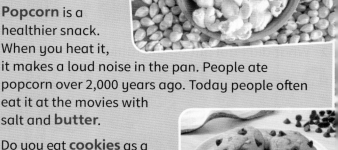

ALL BLOGS   MY BLOG   NEW POST

Kid's Box Reports

People from different countries eat different kinds of food. Some dishes are famous all over the world.

Food

Sushi is a cold Japanese **dish**. You can make sushi with rice and fish that isn't cooked. You eat sushi with **chopsticks**.

In Italy they eat a lot of **pizza** and **pasta** dishes. There are a lot of different kinds of pasta and **sauces**. Two of the most famous are spaghetti and macaroni.

Paella is Spanish. It's a rice dish, and it's also the name of the **pan** you use. People make it with chicken or seafood. It's delicious!

A **snack** is a small meal or something light to eat between meals. What's your favorite snack? The doughnut, a small ring or ball of fried dough, is famous all over the world, but it originally came from Germany and the Netherlands.

Popcorn is a healthier snack. When you heat it, it makes a loud noise in the pan. People ate popcorn over 2,000 years ago. Today people often eat it at the movies with salt and **butter**.

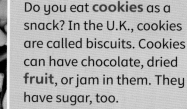

Do you eat **cookies** as a snack? In the U.K., cookies are called biscuits. Cookies can have chocolate, dried **fruit**, or jam in them. They have sugar, too.

Peanut butter and **jam** sandwiches are popular in the U.S.A. Peanut butter isn't made from milk. It's made from **peanuts**. We cook fruit and sugar at a high temperature to make jam.

---

2 **Read again and say "yes" or "no." Correct the wrong sentences.**

1 Sushi is made from bread and sauce.
2 You eat sushi with spoons.
3 Paella is the name of a dish and a pan.
4 Doughnuts originally came from France.
5 Peanut butter and jam sandwiches are popular in North America.
6 Jam is made from fruit and peanuts.
7 "Biscuit" is another word for "cookie."
8 People often eat popcorn at the movies.

3 **Talk to a partner.**

1 Have you ever eaten any of these kinds of food? Which one is your favorite?

> I have eaten sushi, doughnuts, cookies, and popcorn. My favorite is sushi!

2 What is your favorite snack and when do you eat it?

> My favorite snack is pears, and I eat one every day.

1 Read and order the pictures.

I feel hungry.
What can I eat?
Cheese and salad.
Fish and meat.

a

Whoa, too many cookies,
You know it's not good.
Snack on fruit and vegetables,
You know you should.

b

Or a big Italian pizza.
Mmm! That's nice!
Ooh, pasta and sauce,
Or a bowl of rice.

c

Sushi with chopsticks?
Or cereal with a spoon?
I eat sushi with my fingers.
Let's eat soon!

d

It isn't time for lunch,
I know what we can do.
I'm really hungry, Dad!
I'll make a snack for me and you.

1

Is there enough peanut butter?
There's enough strawberry jam.
Are you going to make a sandwich?
Yes, I am.
Ooh! Thanks, Dad!

e

2 🎧 ▶ 33–34 Listen and check.
Do karaoke.

3 Write four sentences. Use the words in the boxes. Play "food bingo."

| There's too much | There isn't enough |
| There are too many | There aren't enough |

burgers   butter   chopsticks   cookies
jam   olives   pasta   pepper   rice
salt   sandwiches   sausages   snacks

4 Read and choose the right words.

Last Saturday, Katy decided to make spaghetti with meat sauce, her favorite (1) _Italian_ pasta (2) _____ .

First, she put some cold water and some (3) _____ into a big pot to boil. When the water was (4) _____ , she put the spaghetti into it to cook.

While this was cooking, she made the (5) _____ for it. She (6) _____ some onions with meat and (7) _____ . She added some (8) _____ , but she put in (9) _____ !

When it was ready, she put the spaghetti onto a big plate and put the sauce on top. When she put her (10) _____ into her mouth to taste it, it was too salty and it tasted terrible!

1	French	Spanish	(Italian)
2	plate	dish	bowl
3	tea	jam	salt
4	hot	corn	cold
5	snack	sandwich	sauce
6	cooks	cooked	cooking
7	bananas	tomatoes	potatoes
8	sugar	salt	jam
9	too many	enough	too much
10	plate	fork	cup

5 Which meal or snack would you like to make? Tell a partner how to make it.

6 📝 Write about your favorite meal or snack. Write 30–40 words.

Sounds and life skills

Exploring food from other cultures

 Watch the video. How do they feel in the cooking class?

Pronunciation focus

 35 Listen and underline the strong words. Then practice with a partner.

ROBERT: So, we have too much sugar and too many apples.

We don't have enough flour or eggs.

What are we going to do?

 36 Listen and write. Say some more examples.

A: We're having a picnic, but ...

B: We have too many _____ and too much _____.

C: And we don't have any _____!

B: What are we going to do?

 Look at the blog post. Do you know these foods? Where is your favorite food from?

My food journey around the world!

One of the great things about travel is the food. Here are some of my favorite dishes ... from Morocco, Japan, Turkey, and Venezuela!

 In a group, discuss food from different countries. Make notes.

Country	Food	Ingredients
France	tarte Tatin	apples

Useful language

So, let's ...
Where is/are ... from?
If you want, we can ...
Cool, why not?

Sounds and life skills: strong words | collaboration

Diggory Bones

🎧 37 ▶

That's all, Richard. You can go now. Go on! Leave!

What do you want from us? Where's the Sun Stone?

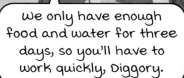

Oh! Too many questions!

We only have enough food and water for three days, so you'll have to work quickly, Diggory.

Why do you need the Sun Stone, Iyam?

I don't need it. I need YOU. I'll tell you where it is when you finish this job for me.

You know there are secret caves under the Pyramid of the Sun, don't you?

And what are we going to find there? Aztec gold?

I think so. There are pictures of corn on the Sun Stone and on the walls here.

Yes. Corn was the most important food for the mayas and the Aztecs.

We both know that corn was their symbol for gold.

I think we'll eat now. That's interesting! I didn't know the Aztecs ate gold.

I knew that they ate chocolate with pepper. Would you like some?

No!

And insects, too.

Stop it! Quetzalcóatl gave corn to the Aztecs! The door to the caves is about three kilometers east of ...

Don't jump, Greedy! The ground's moving!

STOMP
STOMP

Don't move or you'll go down faster! Emily, get me a big knife!

I can't get out! Help me!

 Why will Diggory have to work quickly? Name three things the Aztecs ate.

How does food get to your table?

 ## Amazing apples

What are apples?

We all know that apples are a kind of fruit that grows on trees. They are round, mostly sweet, crunchy, and delicious! In fact, apples have been part of our diet for thousands of years, and it's easy to understand why. We can eat them **raw** as snacks and use them to make juice, sauces, desserts, and salads. They taste amazing, and they're very healthy, too. Apples are full of **vitamins** and **minerals**, and a lot of these vitamins are in the **skin**, so don't peel your apples!

Where do apples grow?

Apples grow in a **mild** climate. This means they need warm summers and cool winters. The first apple trees grew in Central Asia, but now you can find them all over the world, and China is the country that produces the most apples. Farmers plant apple trees in an **orchard**, which is an area of land where fruit trees grow. Did you know there are 7,500 different types of apples around the world? Do you have a favorite type?

The next time you eat an apple, think about where it came from and how it got to you.

Apples really are amazing!

How do apples grow?

An apple tree grows flowers in the spring, and inside each flower there are **seeds**. When insects **pollinate** the flowers, the seeds grow into apples. It takes between four and five months for the apples to be ready to eat, so **harvest time** is usually in late summer or fall. Some countries even celebrate Apple Day around that time of year.

 Apples float in wate this's becau 25% of an a is air!

2   **Read again and match.**

1	A place where fruit trees grow.	d
2	The part of the apple that gives it its color.	
3	The time of year when fruit is ready to eat.	
4	Good things in food that help keep people healthy.	
5	Weather that's not too hot and not too cold.	
6	New plants can grow from these.	
7	To carry pollen between flowers to make seeds grow.	

a   vitamins and minerals
b   mild
c   pollinate
d   an orchard
e   harvest time
f   skin
g   seeds

3   **Do apples grow in your country? How often do you eat or cook with apples?**

Apples grow here – we have some apple trees in our backyard.

I love baking apple pie with my grandma.

FIND OUT MORE
Why can't we eat apple seeds?

1 **Read the article. Why do they move apples on water?**

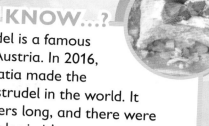

HOW DO APPLES GET TO OUR TABLE?

Apples grow in orchards in countries with mild climates. In late summer and autumn, it is time to harvest them. First, fruit pickers pick the apples and put them into wooden boxes, which are called crates. Then the fruit pickers put the crates onto trucks, and the truck drivers take them to a sorting and packing building.

When they arrive, the apples float into the building on water. The water washes the apples and transports them safely, so they aren't damaged.

Next, the apples pass under a scanner that checks them for color, roundness, and damage. People use this information to sort the apples into different types.

After that, they pack the apples into new crates and store them in big, refrigerated rooms.

When they are ready for selling, people check them one last time. They put a sticker on each apple and pack them by hand. Finally, delivery drivers deliver the crates of apples to supermarkets in trucks.

2 **Underline examples of sequencing words in the article in Activity 1.**

3 **In pairs, discuss where your favorite foods come from and what they are made of. Make notes in your notebook.**

Which food?   Where does it come from?

What do you need to do before you can eat it?

Learning to write:
Sequencing words

We use words like *first*, *next*, *then*, and *finally* to show how to do something in the correct order.

First, the apples are picked.
Then the truck drivers take them to a packing building.

Ready to write:

Go to Workbook page 42.

Project

Write a recipe using apples.

Biology: apples |  critical thinking **43**

1 🎧 39 **Listen and draw lines. There is one example.**

Helen   Katy   Harry   Michael   Richard   Sarah   William

2 **Ask and answer.**

What's the name of the restaurant?

It's …

3 Play the game.

Snakes and ladders

Instructions: Throw a dice and move around the board. When you land on a square with words, make a correct sentence. If you are right, go UP the ladder. DON'T go down the snake. If you are wrong, DON'T go up the ladder. Go DOWN the snake.

73

74 when we walk in woods, we see bird

75

76

77

78

79 she have picnic when she see bear

80

FINISH

72

71

70

69 I make pizza when my sister come in

68

67

66

65

64

56

57

58

59

60 when he swim in lake, kick a rock

61

62

63

54 when he cross bridge, my dad fall in river

53

52 when I climb mountain, I break leg

51

50

49

48

47

46

43 it snow when we get to forest

37

38

39

40

41

42

44

45

36

35

34

33 they sail boat when storm begin

32

31

30

29

28

19 you have breakfast when I call

20

21

22

23

24 when we put up tent, it start to rain

25

26

27

10 I drink milk when Mom arrive

18

17

16

15

14

13

12

11

1 START

2

3 when I eat sandwich, phone ring

4

5

6

7

8

9

5 Under the ocean

1 ▶ **What have the people found on the beach? Watch and check.**

2 ▶ **Watch again and answer the questions.**

1 Have they talked about the next blog post for two weeks or two days? For two weeks.
2 Has the rescue team been there since ten o'clock or since seven o'clock?
3 What have they done to help the dolphin?
4 Who hasn't seen a dolphin before?
5 Has the dolphin eaten anything?
6 How does the dolphin get back into the water?

STUDY

We **still haven't chosen** a topic.
The rescue team **has been** there **since** ten o'clock.
The dolphin**'s been** there **for** about three hours.

3 **Read and match.**

1 I've never seen   a there for two hours.
2 The rescue team has been   b project for three days.
3 The dolphin has been on the   c since half past ten.
4 The children have been in the kitchen   d a dolphin before.
5 They still haven't   e sand since nine o'clock.
6 We've worked on the   f thought of a topic.

4 **Ask and answer.**

1 Why does the dolphin need help? What do the people do to help it?
2 What else can we do to help fish and other animals that live in the ocean?

Language: present perfect with *for, since, still*

1 ▶ **Can you remember the last lesson? Watch the language video.**

2 **Read and look at the pictures. Mark (✓) the things he has done.**

I've been at the beach since half past ten.
I've picked up shells next to the ocean.
I've walked in the water, and I've touched it with my hand.
I've found tide pools, and I've played with the sand.
I still haven't seen a dolphin or a whale.
I still haven't ridden in a boat with a sail.
I still haven't caught a fish to eat
Or met a mermaid without any feet.
But I've sat on my towel, felt the sun on my face,
And I've thought that this is my favorite place.
I've watched the birds as they've flown in the air.
I've eaten a sandwich, an apple, and a pear.
I've swum with my friends, made castles with my dad.
It's one of the best days that I've ever had!
We've been here for hours, now it's time to go.
I love the beach, that's all I need to know.

3 🎧 ▶ 40–41 **Listen and check. Do karaoke.**

4 **Ask and answer.**

> Has he played with the sand?
> Yes, he has.

> Has he sailed in a boat?
> No, he hasn't.

5 **Look at Michael's timeline. Make ten sentences: five with "since" and five with "for."**

2012	2018	2019	2020	2021
was born in Atlanta, Georgia	started Atlanta Elementary School	learned to play tennis	started to learn French	got a racing bike

1 Michael / live / in Atlanta
2 Michael / study / at Atlanta Elementary School
3 Michael / play tennis
4 Michael / study French
5 Michael / have his racing bike

6 📝 **Draw and write your timeline.**

7 **Tell a partner about your timeline.**

> I've lived here since 2014.

Practice: present perfect with *for, since, still*   **47**

ALL BLOGS   MY BLOG   NEW POST

Kid's Box Reports

We still haven't explored our **oceans** completely, but here are some interesting ocean animals of different shapes and **sizes**.

Ocean animals

Seals live in the ocean and on land, like **turtles**, but they don't lay eggs! They are **mammals**, so they have babies and feed them milk.

Coral reefs look like forests, but corals aren't plants. Each reef is millions of very small animals. The reefs are important because a lot of other ocean animals live there.

This giant Japanese spider **crab** has lived in the ocean since the time of the dinosaurs. It's 4 m across. It has two **claws** and eight thin legs with white spots.

This blue-ringed **octopus** lives on coral reefs close to Australia. It's very small (6 cm), but it's very dangerous.

Like crabs, **lobsters** have a hard **shell** and two big claws, but their bodies aren't round.

Like an octopus, a **squid** has eight "legs." This is a giant squid. They can be 14 m long, and they have the biggest eyes in the world.

Jellyfish have been in our oceans for 650 million years. They don't have a brain or bones, and they can be from 2.5 cm to 61 m long! They eat small fish and tiny animals called zooplankton.

 2 Read again and answer.

1 Which of these ocean animals is a mammal?
2 How is a crab different from a lobster?
3 Why are coral reefs important?
4 Which ocean animal has lived in the ocean since the time of the dinosaurs?
5 Which ocean animal can be 61 meters long?
6 Which small ocean animal is very dangerous?
7 Which ocean animal has the biggest eyes?
8 Name three ocean animals that have eight legs.

 3 Talk to a partner.

1 Which ocean animal do you think is the most exciting? Why?

> I think the giant squid is the most exciting because it has the biggest eyes in the world.

2 Have you ever seen any of these ocean animals? Which ones and where?

> I have seen seals on a beach near my home.

1 Correct the sentences.

1 People have eaten lobsters since 2,000 years.
2 Jellyfish lived on Earth for millions of years.
3 People have find giant squid in all the world's oceans.
4 There have been coral reefs in our oceans since millions of years.
5 Scientists have found 6,000 different kinds of crabs, but they still hasn't found them all.
6 Seals have swim in our oceans for 22 million years.

2 🎧 42 Listen and write a letter in each box.

What is each person's favorite thing at the aquarium?

Mr. Pepper [b]   Sarah [ ]   Helen [ ]   Richard [ ]   David [ ]   Emma [ ]

 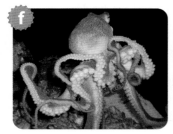  

3 Read the text and write the missing words. Write one word on each line.

We find coral reefs in warm (1) _____water_____ , usually close to land. They are home to a lot of different ocean (2) _____ , like lobsters, turtles, octopuses, and jellyfish. A lot of beautiful (3) _____ live here, too, like the clownfish and the parrotfish. The biggest coral reef (4) _____ the world is the Great Barrier Reef. It is in the ocean close to Australia. Coral reefs (5) _____ in danger because of dirty water and climate change. We need (6) _____ take care of our coral reefs.

4 Play the game.

(It's big and green. It has a hard shell.)   (Is it a turtle?)   (Yes, it is!)

Sounds and life skills
Finding out more

1 ▶ **Watch the video. How do they feel when they see the news?**

Pronunciation focus

2 🎧 43 **Listen and complete. Underline the sounds /p/, /b/, /d/, or /ð/.**

> beach   been   Dad   dolphin   mother   there

EVA: Hi, **(1)** _____ , what's happening **(2)** _____ ?

MR. SHARMA: They've found a **(3)** _____ on the **(4)** _____ .
The rescue team has **(5)** _____ there since ten o'clock. They think it's lost its **(6)** _____ .

3 🎧 44 **Listen and match. Say more sentences with a partner.**

puzzle	in the desert.
They've found a — bat	behind a door.
dinosaur	on the balcony.
violin	in the town.
feather	in the bathroom.

4 **Read the news article. Match the information to the questions.**

Dramatic rescue at Park Drive Beach

(1) At nine o'clock this morning, on Park Drive Beach, **(2)** a father and his son found a dolphin. A team of rescuers has been on the beach **(3)** since ten o'clock this morning. **(4)** They have moved the dolphin onto a blanket and have put water over it. They think it was looking for its mother.
The rescuers have now seen the mother, and **(5)** they are going to take the dolphin out into the ocean.

Where is the dolphin? ☐ 1

Have they been on the beach for a long time? ☐

What are the rescuers going to do? ☐

Who found the dolphin? ☐

What has the team of rescuers done to help it? ☐

5 **In pairs, do a role play.**

Student A
You are a journalist at the beach. Ask questions about the dolphin.

Student B
You were walking on the beach when you saw the dolphin. Answer the questions.

Useful language
What's happening …?
They've found …
What have the … done to help?

Diggory Bones

Quicksand! You should be more careful, Mr. Greedy.

You've pulled these plants, and you've opened this cave.

Quickly!

I've found a flashlight. Come on! Let's go and look at the cave.

I've known about these caves since 1971 — it was a big story in the news! But will this one take us under the Pyramid of the Sun?

Wait for me! That Aztec gold's mine! Mine!

In ancient mythology, this is the place where their gods made the sun, the moon, and the universe.

What does it mean, Dad?

It means that there's been gold here for hundreds of years.

I'll be surprised if there's gold here.

Quetzalcóatl got his long green feathers here.

A turtle shell. The turtle meant both earth and water to …

 Clap! Clap! Clap!

You've given us another great lesson, Bones.

I haven't finished. Turtles were also for people like you, Greedy, hard and strong on the outside, but soft and weak on the inside.

Good one, Dad!

Very funny, Bones. Now, why isn't there any gold?

Because gold wasn't important to the Aztecs. The long green feathers of the Quetzal bird were their greatest treasure.

Richard's using my cell to follow us. I've given him instructions to destroy this old place if you don't help me!

OK. We're at the wrong place. Come on! It'll soon be the longest day.

1 How long has Diggory known about the caves? What instructions has Mr. Greedy given to Richard?

How can we make electricity?

1 **Listen and read. Write the types of energy.**

 **RENEWABLE ENERGY** ➡

For a long time, **energy** has come from **fossil fuels** like coal, oil, and gas. We use fossil fuels to make electricity for our homes, schools, businesses, and transportation. But fossil fuels also cause **pollution**, so they aren't good for our **environment**. In fact, we now understand that fossil fuels are dangerous for our planet.

But can we get energy from other sources? Yes, of course! Energy is all around us, in sunlight, water, and wind. These are natural forms of energy called **renewable energy**, which means we can keep using them for as long as we need.

We're already using renewable energy. Maybe you've seen **wind turbines** in the country, which create **wind energy**.

When the wind blows strongly, it turns the turbines to make electricity.

Solar energy comes from the sun. If you see **solar panels** on the roof of a house, you know the house uses solar energy! Solar panels have **silicon** in them, which is made from sand. When the sun shines on silicon, it creates an electric charge. This means solar panels can make electricity.

Hydro energy comes from water. Flowing water, like in a river, turns large turbines to make electricity. In fact, more than 2,000 years ago, the ancient Egyptians used water to turn big wheels to make flour.

More and more countries are starting to get their energy from nature. One day we'll only use renewable energy, and it will be much healthier for our planet.

1 _____

2 _____

3 _____

2 **Read again and mark (✓).**

	Solar energy (sun)	Wind energy	Hydro energy (water)
1 It's a source of renewable energy.	✓	✓	✓
2 People can make it on their roofs.			
3 It uses turbines.			
4 A material made of sand makes electricity.			
5 It's good for the environment.			

3 **Which types of renewable energy could work well in your country?**

We get a lot of sunshine, so solar energy works well in our country.

 **FIND OUT MORE**
What is geothermal energy?

Environment: renewable energy | 🛡 collaboration

1 Read the essay. Does the writer think tidal energy is a good thing?

The advantages and disadvantages of tidal energy

Introduction
Tidal energy is a type of hydro energy, which means it uses water. Our oceans have tides, so the water levels go up and down twice a day. This movement of the water turns large turbines under the ocean, and that makes electricity.

Advantages
There are a lot of reasons why people think tidal energy is a good idea. Firstly, it's renewable energy, so it doesn't cause pollution. Another reason is we can always make this type of energy because tides don't stop moving.

Disadvantages
On the other hand, a disadvantage of tidal energy is that it's very new. This means it's still very expensive to build the turbines and put them underwater.

Ending
To sum up, I think that tidal energy will be very popular because it will get cheaper as the technology gets better. Renewable energy is important for the future.

The world's biggest tidal energy turbine is ready to go underwater in Scotland!

2 Underline three topic sentences in the essay in Activity 1.

3 In pairs, brainstorm the advantages and disadvantages of renewable energy. Make notes in your notebook.

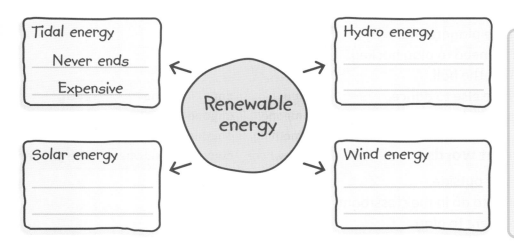

Tidal energy
- Never ends
- Expensive

Renewable energy

Hydro energy

Solar energy

Wind energy

Learning to write:

Topic sentences
We use a topic sentence to introduce a new section of an essay.

There are a lot of reasons why ...

On the other hand ...

To sum up, I think/believe/agree that ...

Ready to write:
Go to Workbook page 52.

Project
Make a poster about renewable energy.

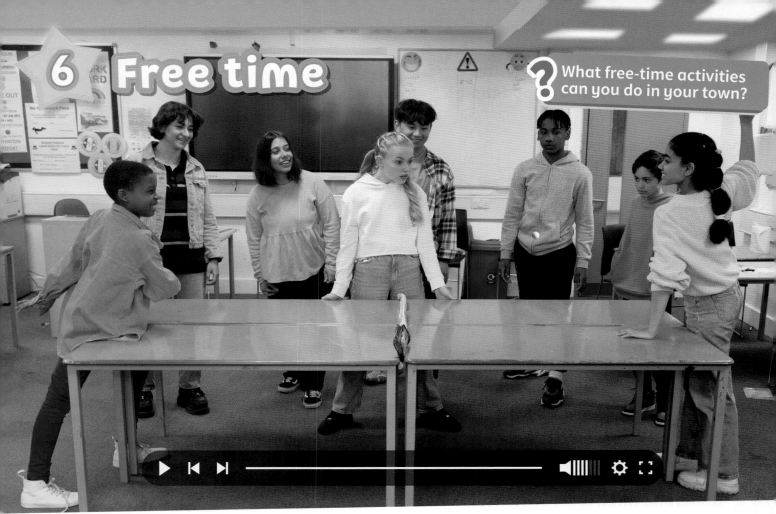

6 Free time

1 ▶ **What do they use to play Ping-Pong? Watch and check.**

2 ▶ **Watch again and correct the sentences.**

1 Everything's dry outside.

> Everything's wet outside.

2 There's nothing to do on the playground.
3 They have everything they need to play hockey.
4 Someone else wants to kick the ball.
5 They have to go somewhere else to dance.
6 They have something to sing about.

3 **Read and choose the right words.**

1 **Everything / Nothing** is wet outside.
2 There's **nothing / anything** to do in the classroom.
3 There's **everywhere / nowhere** to play.
4 They don't have **everywhere / anywhere** to play Ping-Pong.
5 They have **everything / nothing** they need to play.
6 Does **anyone / no one** else want to play?
7 Find **nowhere / somewhere** else to play.
8 Go outside, **everyone / no one**!

STUDY

some	any	no	every
someone	**any**one	**no** one	**every**one
something	**any**thing	**no**thing	**every**thing
somewhere	**any**where	**no**where	**every**where

4 **Ask and answer.**

1 What did you think of Eva's game? Would you like to play it?
2 Have you ever invented a game? What were the rules?

1 ▶ **Can you remember the last lesson? Watch the language video.**

2 **Read and choose the right words.**

○ ○ ○ ○

from: alex360@kidsbox.mail

Dear Robert

Last Saturday my family decided to go (1) **somewhere** / anywhere different for the day. (2) **Something** / **Someone** who works with Dad told him about an exciting new exhibition at the Space Museum. I'd like to be an astronaut when I grow up, so I want to learn (3) **everything** / **nowhere** about space. The exhibition was really interesting. There were (4) **some** / **any** spacesuits that we could try on, but we didn't because there wasn't enough time and we wanted to go to the space theater. We saw an old movie called *Space Jam*. It was really funny, and (5) **nothing** / **everyone** loved it. After the movie, we visited the museum store. We saw models of the Saturn Rocket, but we didn't buy one because there was (6) **no one** / **anywhere** there. Here's a picture. Have you ever seen it in a movie?

There was too much to see in one day, so we couldn't see (7) **anything** / **everything**. At the end, we were tired, and there wasn't (8) **anything** / **anywhere** to sit down, so we went to the restaurant. We had (9) **no one** / **something** to drink before the museum closed at half past five. It was a great day out. What about you? Did you do (10) **anything** / **everyone** interesting last weekend?

All the best,

Alex

3 🎧 47 **Listen and write.**

Kind of show: (1) ___quiz show___
The two children's names:
(2) _____ and (3) _____
The place: somewhere in the (4) _____
The place: (5) _____
How many questions does the boy ask?
(6) _____

4 **Play the game. Say it in ten.**

It's a sport.

Is it something you play with a ball?

Yes, it is.

Is it something you play in a sports center?

No, it isn't.

5 **Ask and answer.**

Do you like playing Ping-Pong?

Find someone who …	Name
1 likes playing Ping-Pong.	Eva
2 goes swimming more than twice a week.	
3 has a hobby different from yours.	
4 can ski.	
5 likes ice-skating.	
6 goes somewhere different from you in their free time.	

Read the blog. How long has Katy had her skateboard?

ALL BLOGS MY BLOG NEW POST

Kid's Box Reports

This month, we've talked to different people about their hobbies.

Hobbies

Fahad enjoys **fashion design**. He makes amazing T-shirts, and a lot of his friends ask him to make T-shirts for them. He **sews** and paints the T-shirts.

Katy's had her **skateboard** for two years, and she can do a lot of exciting **tricks**. She goes to the skatepark to practice jumping with her friends because you should never skateboard close to a street.

Emma's ridden a bike since she was five. She rides her **mountain bike** everywhere, but she enjoys it most when she and her dad go to a special **bike trail**. They can ride up and down hills and through forests.

Holly loves doing **puzzles** and playing **board games**. She plays **chess** with the school club, and she's practicing for a national competition. People have played chess for more than a thousand years.

Peter loves music, but he doesn't **play an instrument**. He uses his mouth to copy the sounds and rhythms of drums. It is called **beatboxing**.

Leon has to be in good shape and strong because he is a **ballet dancer**. He doesn't just dance, he has to learn to jump in different ways and land safely and beautifully. He also has to lift his partner.

 Read again and find these things.

1 something you can wear
2 something you stand on to ride
3 something you sit on to ride
4 somewhere with a lot of trees
5 somewhere you can go to ride
6 something that people have played for centuries
7 something ballet dancers have to learn to do
8 someone who jumps beautifully to dance

 Talk to a partner.

1 Have you tried any of these hobbies? Which ones?

> Yes, I have tried playing board games and beatboxing.

2 Which hobby do you think is the most difficult? Why?

> I think ballet dancing is the most difficult because you have to lift your partner.

1 **Read and complete.**

> beatbox   bike   chess   climb   cut   design   everyone   ~~hobbies~~
> learn   park   sing   ski   something   somewhere   watch

Free time, free time. Lots of (1) _____hobbies_____ **to do.**
There's something for (2) _____ **. There's** (3) _____ **for you.**

You can do anything in your free time.
You can learn to skate, you can learn to (4) _____ .
You can skateboard in a (5) _____ or (6) _____ in the snow.
You can (7) _____ some clothes: draw, (8) _____ , and sew.

You can learn to play (9) _____ , if that's what you like.
You can learn to sail or ride a mountain (10) _____ .
You can learn about music: play it or (11) _____ ,
Pop, rap, or (12) _____ . Enjoy everything.

You can (13) _____ movies or act in a play.
You can walk in the hills and (14) _____ to find your way.
You'll have (15) _____ to go and something to do.
You'll make new friends who like the same things as you.

Chorus

2 48–49 **Listen and check. Do karaoke.**

3 **Invent another verse. Use these words or your own ideas.**

> camp   cars   cook   dance   golf   hockey   make   mix   planes
> play soccer / baseball   sled   surf   swim   take pictures   tennis   weights

4 **Read the definitions. What hobby is it?**

1 This is something you can do in your free time. You do it with a board that is usually made of wood, and you can do it in a special park.

2 This hobby is a type of music, but it isn't singing. You play music without an instrument. You use your mouth and your body to make the sounds.

3 You can play this anywhere, but you need a board and pieces. People usually sit down when they play it.

5 **Write more definitions for a partner to guess.**

It's something ...
Everyone can ...

Practice: hobbies   57

Sounds and life skills
Imagining and inventing

 1 ▶ **Watch the video. How and why do Robert's feelings change?**

Pronunciation focus

 2 🎧 50 **Listen. Which question is more polite?**

EVA: Sally, can I borrow a book, please?

BOY: Sally, can I borrow a book, please?

3 🎧 51 **Listen and complete. Practice with a partner. Say some more examples.**

A: Can I borrow your _____ , please?

B: Yes, _____ .

A: Thank you.

 4 **Read the blog. How many game ideas are there? Circle what you need.**

BOREDOM BUSTERS!

If you can't think of anything to do on a rainy day, invent your own games!

We used some books for a net and two books for paddles to play Ping-Pong! But you can invent your own games! Play boot basketball, for example! Find some old boots and write numbers on them. Then, throw bottle caps into the boots and score points! Or ... use your boots for a boot-throwing competition outside! How far can you throw them?

Happy inventing. Have fun!

 5 📝 **In a group, discuss ways to use old things. Make notes.**

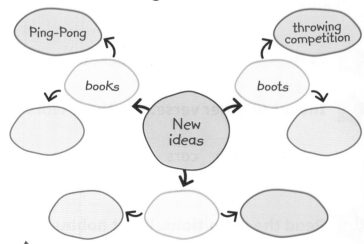

Ping-Pong

throwing competition

books

boots

New ideas

 6 **Compare your ideas. Choose a game to demonstrate.**

Useful language

I have an idea!   We can use ... to ...
...'s invented a game.

Diggory Bones

52

We have to go somewhere closer to the ocean. The Aztecs expected Quetzalcóatl to come back to them by sea.

Let's go then! We don't have much time.

A corn symbol will take me to a cave of gold. Where are we going?

We're going to Kukulcán's pyramid at Chichén Itzá. It'll take two days to get there.

Kukulcán's the mayan word for Quetzalcóatl. He was the god who gave them corn, remember?

Who's Kukulcán, Bones? What's the connection with corn?

That's right. The arts were very important to the mayas. There was a special god for the ball game and the arts.

Look, everyone! Here's a dance for the gods! I can't see any caves of gold anywhere.

It's his most important temple. It's called "the Castle." There'll be corn symbols everywhere ...

... and snake symbols. Look! The Pleiades! The mayas thought they looked like an angry snake's tail!

Wow! This is where the mayas played their famous ball game.

Yes, and before the game, didn't they have music with instruments made of wood and shells?

STOMP STOMP

Twice a year, you can see the form of a snake on the north stairs.

Up the stairs in march, and down again in September. They knew so much about the sun and light.

Bah! Nonsense!

When someone does something to make the gods angry, the pyramid sounds like a Quetzal bird singing.

Bravo! Another boring lesson from Dr. Bones.

Clap! Clap! Clap!

It's nothing to laugh about, mr. Greedy.

What's that noise? Can't anyone else hear it? Aagh!

1 **How often can you see the form of a snake on the north stairs? When does the pyramid sound like a bird singing?**

What makes an amusement park ride exciting and safe?

1 🎧 **53** **Listen and read. Label the photos.**

ALL BLOGS   MY BLOG   NEW POST

Riding the rollercoaster

harness   loops   track   ~~train~~   wheels

Rollercoasters are the most exciting rides at an amusement park. They carry you along on a fast **train**, throwing you around and making you laugh and scream. They're so much fun!

But how do rollercoasters move? Rollercoasters use **gravity**, which is the force that pulls everything down to the ground. Rollercoasters always start with a hill. A motor pulls the train up slowly on a long, straight **track**. After the train reaches the top of the hill, it doesn't use a motor and gravity takes control. Gravity pulls the train downward. And, whoosh, the fun starts!

Rollercoasters are fast, with **twists** and **turns**, and some have **loops**, too, which take you **upside down** for even more scary fun! But how does the train stay on the track?

If you look carefully at a rollercoaster's **wheels**, you will see that there are wheels under the track as well as on it so that they lock the train to the track. That means the train can't **fall off**.

Rollercoasters are designed to be scary, but they are actually very safe. Rollercoaster designers understand how to use gravity to push our bodies safely. Also, everyone on a rollercoaster has to wear a **harness** to hold them into their seat. This is especially important when you think about the world's fastest rollercoaster in the U.A.E., which travels at 240 km an hour!

1 _____ train _____
2 _____

3 _____

4 _____

5 _____

2 **Read again and order the stages of a rollercoaster ride.**

a At the top of the hill, the motor stops moving the train. ☐
b When the energy from the hill is finished, the train stops, and the ride is over. ☐
c First, a motor makes the train move up a big hill. ☐ 1
d The train travels so fast that it can even go around loops! ☐
e Gravity pulls the train down the other side of the hill very fast. ☐

3 **Do you like rollercoasters? Why? Where is your favorite rollercoaster?**

I love rollercoasters because I love going fast!

Me too! Going fast is very exciting!

FIND OUT MORE
What's the longest rollercoaster in the world? Where is it?

1 Read the story. Does the writer like rollercoasters?

My first rollercoaster ride

Last summer, I visited my cousins, and the most exciting thing we did was to go to a fantastic theme park. It was much bigger than an amusement park, and we rode on a lot of great rides, like the scary ghost train and the big wheel.

After a while, my cousins asked if I wanted to ride on the rollercoaster. I said yes, but really I felt scared about it. We all sat down and put on our harnesses. Then the little train started moving slowly up a big hill. The noise of the little train moving up the high track made me feel terrified, and I just wanted to get off. When we reached the top, there was a great view of the theme park. It looked beautiful! Suddenly, the train dropped down the other side, and everyone screamed! It was amazing! We twisted and turned and even went upside down!

Finally, the ride was over, and we were all happy. I rode on the fantastic rollercoaster three more times that day, and now rollercoasters are my favorite rides.

DID YOU KNOW...?
The American engineer who designed the first steel rollercoasters hated the rides he designed because he was always sick when he rode on them!

2 Underline the adjectives in the story in Activity 1. What difference do they make to the story?

3 In pairs, describe your favorite rides. Make notes in your notebook.

Ride	What does it do?	How do you feel?

Learning to write:

Adjectives

We use adjectives to make stories more interesting.

The rollercoaster was **fast** and **exciting**.

I felt so **happy**.

Ready to write:

Go to Workbook page 60.

Project

Design an amusement park ride.

1 **Read the email and write the missing words. Write one word on each line.**

Dear Yousef,

How are you? In your last email you asked me about my
(1) _____hobbies_____ , so I'm going to tell you about two of
them: chess and my mountain bike.

I've played chess (2) _____ four years now. I play
with my friends in a club at school. We meet twice a
week, (3) _____ Tuesdays and Thursdays. I really
(4) _____ it because you have (5) _____
think a lot and because there's a lot of action.

My other hobby is (6) _____ my mountain bike
up the bike trails near our house with my brother. I've
included a picture of me on my bike.

Tell me about some of your hobbies.

Best wishes,

Joshua

2 **Look at the pictures. Tell the story.**

3 Play the game.

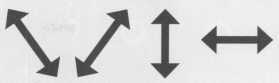

Can you make a sentence?

Instructions: Throw a dice and move around the board. You have to win three verbs in a line:

To win a verb, make a correct sentence using the verb in the present perfect tense.

When you get a verb, cover it with a piece of paper and write your sentence down.

You can land on a square that someone else has won, but you can't win it too!

> I've visited Grandma twice this week.

40 dance	39 sail	38 snow	37	36 comb
31 ski	32 dream	33 plant	34 email	35
30 post	29 burn	28	27 finish	26 jump
21	22 invite	23 arrive	24 rain	25 mix
20 clean	19 glue	18 brush	17 paint	16
11 buy	12	13 study	14 score	15 race
10 drop	9 sled	8 text	7 open	6 start
1 play	2 smile	3	4 visit	5 kick

6

7 Fashion sense

1 ▶ **Why does Robert look like a teacher? Watch and check.**

2 ▶ **Watch again and say "yes" or "no." Correct the wrong sentences.**

1 There's going to be a school contest this week.
2 Eva might wear jeans to the dance.
3 Sally's going to wear her new skirt.
4 Eva thinks Robert might want to change his pants.
5 Robert's clothes may look better with a jacket.
6 It isn't cold. Robert might not need a jacket.
7 Sally feels like a rock star.
8 They decide to write about movies and music for the blog post.

> No. There's going to be a school dance this week.

STUDY

I think it **may** look better with a jacket.
You **may** feel like a rock star.
I **might not** need a jacket.

3 Read and order the words.

1 might / a / Eva / T-shirt. / wear / jeans and
2 jacket? / wear / Who / a / might
3 not / wear / I / a sweater / tonight. / might

4 hot / may / a jacket. / be too / It / to wear
5 a shirt. / Robert / wear / might
6 lot at / They / the dance. / might / dance a

4 Ask and answer.

1 What did you think of Robert's fashion choices? Did you like any of his clothes?
2 What clothes might you wear to a school dance or party?

1 **Can you remember the last lesson? Watch the language video.**

2 **Look at the pictures. Read and match.**

a I'm sorry, Peter. We may not have time. I have a lot to do this afternoon.
b I don't know. I might wear my sweatshirt, or I might wear my jacket.
c I think I might, or I may wear a skirt.
d She says she might come, but she needs to finish her homework first.

1 — What are you going to wear to watch soccer?

2 — Are you going to wear your new pants to the party?

3 — Is Clara going to come to the dance on Friday?

4 — Can we go to the park on our way home, please?

3 **Practice the conversations with a partner. Write another conversation together.**

4 **Write questions with "might."**

1 When / go / dance?
2 What clothes / wear / dance?
3 What music / dance to / dance?
4 Who / take / pictures of?
5 Who / go with?
6 What / take / with you?

1 When might you go to
the dance?

5 **Ask and answer.**

When might you go to the dance?

I think I might go next week.

6 **Play the game. What's in the bag? Write sentences with "may."**

It may be a scarf.

Read the blog. What two things did people do differently a long time ago?

ALL BLOGS   MY BLOG   NEW POST

Kid's Box Reports

Fashions may come and go, but some fashion extras haven't changed for centuries.

Fashion

Buttons hold clothes together and **decorate** them. Today buttons are made of plastic, metal, glass, and shells, but the ancient Greeks had buttons made of gold.

Did you know that the first **umbrellas protected** people from the sun? Now there are big golf umbrellas and small, **light** umbrellas that we can carry in a purse.

Your grandfather probably wore **shorts** to school until he was 12! These days we usually wear them for sports and when it's very hot.

People usually wear **gloves** on their hands when it's cold, but some people use gloves at work, for example, firefighters.

Men and women have worn **belts** for about 5,000 years. People first used them to carry things and, much later, to hold their pants up.

The first **pockets** were small bags that people wore on their belts. Thieves could take them easily, so people put the bags inside their clothes. Then it was difficult to get money out of them, so in the 18th century, people sewed pockets into their clothes.

Women and girls wear **tights** under their skirts and dresses to cover their legs in cold weather. Tights can be **thin** and light or **thick** and **heavy**. They are usually made of **nylon** or wool.

 Read again and complete.

1 The ancient Greeks had gold __buttons__ .
2 The first umbrellas protected people from the _____ .
3 Older boys wore _____ to school 60 years ago.
4 _____ protect our hands.
5 People wear _____ to hold their pants up.
6 The first pockets were small _____ .
7 People sewed _____ into their clothes 300 years ago.
8 _____ are usually made of nylon or wool.

 Talk to a partner.

1 Which clothes do you prefer when you want to be comfortable?

> I prefer jeans and a T-shirt when I want to be comfortable.

2 Which clothes do you think are the most fashionable?

> I think jeans are the most fashionable.

66   Vocabulary: fashion and adjectives

1 Read and match.

1 It's very hot today.
2 My pants are falling down.
3 Look at those black clouds.
4 I can't find my money.
5 Hey, I like your striped tights!
6 The cook has really big gloves.

a They stop her from burning her hands.
b He's wearing a T-shirt and shorts.
c They look great with that skirt.
d I need a belt!
e It isn't in my pocket!
f I might take my umbrella.

2 Read and say the words.

There's a great new dance
And we do it at school.
School dance! School dance!

Turn to the .

Turn to the .

Turn around and around.

Dance **and** .

School dance!

Long striped ,

Big polka-dot .

 and ,

And beautiful .

 and ,

and ,

Walking around
Like queens and kings.
School dance!

Big square ,

 and ,

 and .

The clothes that we love.

Chorus
School dance!

3  54–55 Listen and check. Do karaoke.

4 Play the game. Who is it?

He's wearing gray shorts.

It might be *i*.

No! He's wearing …

Sounds and life skills
Planning together

Come on! Hurry up!

1 **Watch the video. How is Robert feeling?**

Pronunciation focus

2 56 **Listen and write. Then draw lines for connected speech.**

ROBERT: Does this _____ OK?

EVA: You might want to change your shirt.

ROBERT: _____ about this?

EVA: Yeah! _____ OK! But I _____ it may look better _____ a jacket.

3 57 **Listen and complete. Practice with a partner.**

A: Let's plan _____ school dance. What does _____ think?

B: Let's put _____ of balloons.

C: We might _____ to play music _____ .

4 58 **Look. Listen and circle.**

5 **In a group, plan your own school dance and make notes.**

School dance

Place: **playground / art room**

Date: **Friday, May 10th / Thursday, May 10th**

Time: **7:00 – 9:00 p.m. / 6:00 – 8:00 p.m.**

Theme: **sports heroes / famous musicians**

Decorations: **gold and silver / white and black** balloons

Music: **dance / rock 'n' roll**

Food: **spaghetti / pizza**

School dance

Place: _____

Date: _____

Time: _____

Theme: _____

Decorations: _____

Music: _____

Food: _____

Useful language

We might want to …

How about …?

Orange balloons may be better.

Sounds and life skills: connected speech | collaboration

Diggory Bones

🎧 59 ▶

That was a great joke, Dad. Did you see his face?

The Mayas designed this to sound like a Quetzal bird when someone clapped.

You look like you've seen an Aztec brave.

The braves painted their faces and wore birds' feathers and animal fur. Everyone who saw them felt afraid.

Quetzalcóatl was also the god of learning. You might learn something from this adventure.

And you might be sorry for your joke.

This is a giant calendar. There are stairs on each face: north, south, east, and west, each with 91 steps.

And the top step makes 365. One for each day of the year, but I think we've missed something.

That round building's where the mayas watched the sky. We may see something from there.

We have to move fast. We don't have much time.

If you're wrong, I'm going to be very unhappy, Bones.

Hmm. The sun'll be at its highest point soon.

When these bowls are full of water, they work like mirrors. The Mayas used them to watch the sky better.

What?

Quickly! We have some bottles of water here. We need to put some into the bowls.

It's almost 11:28, when the sun's at its highest. Let's see what happens now.

Richard's following us, remember? No tricks!

Come on! There it is! That picture will open the secret door to the gold.

It might not take us to gold, mr. Greedy.

 1 **How many steps are there on each face of the pyramid? What time is the sun at its highest?**

What happens to our old sneakers?

1 🎧 60 **Listen and read. Give two examples of eco-friendly sneakers.**

The journey of sneakers

Sneakers, tennis shoes, sports shoes, running shoes – whatever you call them, they're shoes that people wear for sports and fashion. But have you ever looked at your sneakers and thought about where they came from?

People started wearing sneakers about 150 years ago. They were more comfortable than other shoes because they had **rubber soles**. In the early 1900s, people wore sneakers for sports, but by the 1950s, young people were wearing sneakers for fashion, too.

Fashion sneakers were very popular by the 1980s! New, colorful designs made sneakers more popular with young people. Inventions like **Velcro**, instead of **laces**, and new technology like **air cushions** made sneakers more comfortable than ever!

Sustainable sneakers

Most sneakers are made of materials like rubber, plastic, or leather, which can take a long time to **decompose** after we throw them away. This is bad for the environment. Plastic, for example, can take more than 500 years to decompose!

Making one pair of sneakers also makes about 14 kg of **carbon emissions**. So, when 24 billion pairs of shoes are made every year, that's a lot of **pollution**!

To be more **eco-friendly**, many companies are using new materials for their sneakers. In some stores, you can now buy sneakers that are made of **plant-based materials**, like pineapples, grapes, sugarcane, cotton, and mushrooms! These materials decompose more quickly, so they're much better for the environment.

Other companies make sneakers out of recycled products, like plastic bottles, old fishing nets, and trash from the oceans.

One thing is for sure: we love our sneakers! So, will sustainable sneakers be our shoes of the future?

 2 Read again and correct the mistakes.

1 The first sneakers had ~~leather~~ soles. _____rubber_____

2 In the 1950s, young people started wearing sneakers for sports. _____

3 In the 1980s, some sneakers had Velcro instead of air cushions. _____

4 Most sneakers made of plastic, rubber, or leather decompose very quickly. _____

5 Eco-friendly companies want to use plastic materials to make sustainable sneakers. _____

 3 Do you have a favorite pair of sneakers? Why do you like them?

> I love my sneakers because they have air cushions in them, so they're really comfortable!

> I have different sneakers to wear when I'm not playing sports. They're fashionable!

 FIND OUT MORE
What are the most expensive sneakers in the world?

1 **Read the brochure. Which parts give information? Which parts give advice?**

DID YOU KNOW...?

In the past, right and left shoes had the same shape! Then in 1892, an American company started making the first sneakers with a right and left shoe, and they were a big success!

How to give your sneakers a longer life

Do you ever think about what happens to your sneakers when you throw them away? Did you know that about 90% of your old shoes end up as trash? The trash takes hundreds of years to decompose.

One company has a great way to use old sneakers – it recycles them by cutting them up into tiny pieces and using them on sports fields and running tracks.

Here are some ideas to make your sneakers last longer:

- You could make your sneakers last longer by taking them off correctly. Always untie the laces and don't step on the backs.
- Don't wear the same sneakers every day – you could wear different ones.
- If your sneakers are dirty, clean them with an old toothbrush.
- If they're wet, put newspaper inside them to dry them.
- You could take your sneakers to a second-hand store when you're done with them.

2 **Underline examples of "could" and "if" in the brochure in Activity 1.**

3 **In pairs, discuss how to give an item of clothing a longer life.**

- Item of clothing
- What is it made of?
- Ideas for giving it a longer life

Learning to write:

could and *if*

We use *could* and *if* to make suggestions or give ideas.

You **could** buy clothes made of recycled materials.

If your jeans are too small, make them into a bag.

Ready to write:

Go to Workbook page 70.

Project

Design a pair of sneakers that are good for the environment.

8 Around the world

Which countries do you want to visit?

1 ▶ Where are the other winners from? Watch and check.

2 ▶ Watch again. Order the sentences.

1 They've just given the names of the blog competition winners. ☐
2 I've just cleaned my desk. ☐
3 I've started it, but I haven't finished it yet. ☐
4 Have you found any good photos? ☐
5 We've just won new tablets for everyone. ☐ 1
6 Have you written the article on Mexico yet? ☐
7 I haven't saved the article yet. ☐
8 I've already found four good photos. ☐

STUDY
Have you **written** the article **yet**?
I **haven't saved** the article **yet**.
I've **already found** four photos.
I've **just cleaned** my desk.

3 Read and match.

1 Have you spoken to your
2 I've just spent
3 I haven't met
4 I've just found out some
5 Frank's already
6 She's just sent an email

a interesting things about India.
b the new French teacher yet.
c finished school.
d ten dollars on a new T-shirt.
e to her sister in Japan.
f mom about the field trip yet?

4 Ask and answer.

1 Have you cleaned your bedroom this week?
Why or why not?
2 Have you ever won a prize?
What was it for?

72 **Language:** present perfect with *just, yet, already*

1 **Can you remember the last lesson? Watch the language video.**

2 **Read and complete.** been ~~begun~~ bought done packed played put cleaned

We've just finished school,
Our vacation's (1) ___begun___.
We've (2) _____ our last test,
Now we're going to have fun.
We've just (3) _____ away our books,
And we've (4) _____ our desks.
So we're all going home. It's time to take a break!

**Yes, it's vacation time! Time to take a break.
Yes, it's vacation time, and we're all feeling great!**

We've (5) _____ in the park,
And we've (6) _____ to the zoo.
We've already (7) _____
Some summer clothes, too.
But we haven't (8) _____ our suitcase,
And we're going to go away
To swim in the ocean and sleep and play all day.

Chorus

3 61–62 **Listen and check. Do karaoke.**

4 **Read and choose the right words.**

○ ○ ○

Hi Sarah,

How are you? I've been in Australia
(1) **just / for / already** a week now, but I haven't seen a kangaroo (2) **since / just / yet**!

We've (3) **just / yet / for** left Sydney, and we're driving to the beach. We've (4) **since / already / yet** seen Sydney Harbour Bridge and the Opera House, but we haven't seen the famous coral reef (5) **yet / already / for**. We'll visit it tomorrow. I can't wait! I've (6) **yet / since / already** taken a hundred pictures, and we've only been here (7) **for / just / since** seven days!

How is your vacation? I haven't heard from you (8) **for / since / just** we arrived here. You have to tell me your news!

Love,

Emma

5 **Write the sentences.
Put the words in the correct place.**

1 (already) I've eaten breakfast.
2 (yet) I haven't done my homework.
3 (yet) Have you spoken to your teacher?
4 (just) We've been to the museum.
5 (already) They've written the blog post.

1 I've already eaten breakfast.

6 **Write five things you've done.
Ask a partner.**

I've ...
1 flown a kite.   4 eaten octopus.
2 swum with dolphins.   5 drunk mango juice.
3 ridden a horse.

7 **Tell another partner.**

Juan's already flown a kite. He hasn't swum with dolphins yet.

Practice: present perfect with *just, yet, already*   **73**

ALL BLOGS   MY BLOG   NEW POST

Kid's Box Reports

Well, this is our last blog post this year. We've won the prize to write for the international blog, so today we're going to tell you about some of the other countries in the competition.

Countries

In **India**, they speak 22 official languages, but Hindi and English are the two most important languages. **Indian** people love movies! In Bollywood they make more movies a year than in Hollywood in the U.S.A.

Mexico is in North America, but **Mexican** people have spoken Spanish for hundreds of years. More people speak **Spanish** in Mexico than in **Spain**. Did you know that modern chewing gum first came from trees in Mexico in the 19th century?

More tourists visit **France** than any other country: about 90 million every year. The **French** also have the most famous bike race in the world, which is called the Tour de France.

Brazil is the fifth biggest country in the world. The people from Brazil are **Brazilian**, but they speak Portuguese. Apart from **Portugal** and Brazil, people speak **Portuguese** in five other countries.

China has the biggest population in the world. More than 1.4 billion people live there, and more people speak **Chinese** as their first language than any other language in the world. The Chinese invented paper money and fireworks.

Greece is not an island, but there are about 2,000 **Greek** islands. A lot of the words we use today, like "mathematics" and "telephone," come from Greek.

---

2 **Read again and answer.**

1 What happens in Bollywood?
2 How many languages do they speak in India?
3 How long have Mexicans spoken Spanish?
4 Which country gets the most visitors?
5 What is the world's fifth biggest country?
6 What did the Chinese invent?
7 How many Greek islands are there?
8 Which old language gives us modern words?

3 **Talk to a partner.**

1 Which of these countries would you like to visit? Why?

> I would like to visit Mexico because I can speak Spanish and I love Mexican food.

2 Talk about somewhere nice to visit in your country.

> Barcelona is a great city to visit because it's next to the beach and there's a lot to see.

1 🎧 63 **Listen and mark (✓) the countries you hear.**

India ☐ _____
Mexico ☐ _____
Italy ☐ _____
France ☐ _____
Brazil ☐ _____
Germany ✓ _Berlin_____
Greece ☐ _____
Spain ☐ _____
the U.S.A. ☐ _____
Portugal ☐ _____

 2 🎧 64 **Listen again and write the capital cities.**

 3 **Look and answer.**

1 What is the capital of Spain?
2 Which capital here is the closest to Rome?
3 Which capital here is the farthest south?
4 Which country is Lisbon the capital of?
5 Which capital here is the farthest east?
6 How many capitals here are north of Paris?

 4 **Read and correct the sentences.** **8**

Archie Mendes is the smartest boy in Europe. His mother's Greek, but his father's Portuguese, so he speaks both of these languages perfectly. He also speaks English, which he's spoken since he was three, and French.

He's only 14 years old, but he's studied at the Sorbonne University in Paris for two years. He's just helped some engineers design an amazing new car that goes on land and on water.

He loves traveling, and he's already been to India and Mexico, but he hasn't been to Brazil yet. He's had an invitation to visit a friend, so he's going to go there for his summer vacation.

He's just come back from Bollywood, where he helped make a new movie. He likes doing a lot of different things in his free time, but his favorite hobby is free running. He's just made a short video. In it, we can see him running through streets and jumping from wall to wall beautifully. He knows he always has to wear special clothes to protect his body when he does it. That's what makes him the smartest boy in Europe!

1 Archie's parents are Chinese and Portuguese.
2 Archie speaks Greek, Portuguese, Spanish, and French.
3 He's spoken English since he was five.
4 He's studied in the capital of Spain for two years.
5 He's just helped some engineers design an amazing new boat that goes on land and on water.
6 He's already been to India, but he hasn't been to Mexico yet.
7 He's only 14, but he's already helped make a car and a TV show.
8 He's just made a short video on long jumping.

Sounds and life skills
Understanding responsibilities

1 ▶ **Watch the video. How do the girls feel? Why?**

Pronunciation focus

2 🎧 65 **Listen and underline the stressed words. Then practice with a partner.**

EVA: I've already found four good photos, but I need two more. Have you written the article on Mexico yet?

SALLY: I've started it, but I haven't finished it yet. Oh, Robert! I've just cleaned my desk. Be careful!

3 🎧 66 **Listen and write. Underline the stressed words. Say some more examples.**

A: Have you _____ your _____ yet?
B: Yes, I've just _____ it.
C: Yes, I've already _____ it.
D: No, I haven't _____ it yet.

4 **Read the article. What responsibilities does David have on the farm?**

My responsibilities on a farm in Mexico

Today we find out about the responsibilities of a farm worker.

David, what's a typical day for you?

Well, you know farmers need to get up very early to feed the animals. The cows are always hungry! We make sure we order enough food in the winter for them until spring. Every day, we milk the cows and collect the eggs from the chickens.

Do you drive a tractor?

Yes. We have sheep, but they aren't on the farm. I drive to their fields to check they have water. Every week, I help the farmer move the sheep to a different field.

Do you also pick fruit or grow vegetables?

I sometimes help in the summer, but that's not really my job.

5 **In pairs, discuss different jobs and their responsibilities.**

> astronaut   chef
>
> journalist   pirate
>
> president   teacher

Useful language

What do you do?
What's a typical day for you?
Do you have to …?
Do you need to …?

Sounds and life skills: stressed words | 🛡 critical thinking

Diggory Bones

I've just pushed the corn symbol! Why hasn't the door opened?

Because you haven't danced for the gods yet.

Do we have to do a dance?

Do we, Dad?

No. We have to push the right symbol.

About four kilometers west of Chichén Itzá, there are some caves called Balankanché.

But the museum there has been open for about 40 years. No secrets there, Dad!

The Aztecs and Mayas both used underground rivers to water their fields.

My gold! Where is it?

My gold! My gold!

They also kept their food underground. There's enough corn here to start a business!

It isn't gold, Mr. Greedy, but, yes, it is treasure. People eat corn all over the world except Antarctica.

Here we are! There's a picture of the god of corn and the opening to a cave.

My gold!

Don't you remember? The Aztec name for the Pleiades was "the marketplace."

Yes, and popcorn's good business. It's popular in theaters everywhere! Now let's go!

Hello there, Diggory! I've brought a few friends with me!

Now let's get the Sun Stone back. Call the museum, Son.

 Aagh!

I've made plans for your daughter, Bones. International travel!

Thank you, Iyam, but I've already made plans for all of us.

Thanks, Dad! Have you told Interpol yet? They've wanted this pair for three years.

You weren't the only one with a cell phone, Iyam! They've used mine to follow us here, too!

1 **What has Iyam just done? How have the police found them?**

Which countries do people visit the most?

1 🎧 68 **Listen and read. Write "table," "pie chart," and "bar graph."**

Let's travel the world!

 **Do you like traveling? People travel for a lot of different reasons, sometimes to other parts of their own country and sometimes even to the other side of the world!**

So, what are the most popular countries for people to visit on vacation?

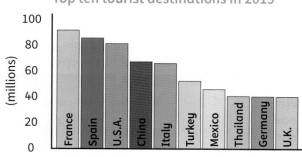

Top ten tourist destinations in 2019

(millions) — France, Spain, U.S.A., China, Italy, Turkey, Mexico, Thailand, Germany, U.K.

When people go on vacation, they usually enjoy going **sightseeing**, doing outdoor activities, and **relaxing** on the beach. We asked a hundred young people about their favorite vacation activities.

Top eight most popular vacation activities

Visiting museums, Sightseeing, Swimming in the ocean, Reading, Relaxing on the beach, shopping, Eating out, Outdoor activities

When we travel **abroad**, we usually need to use a different **currency**. The price of things is different in different countries, too. Some places are more expensive than others.

Prices in different countries

	U.K.	Turkey	U.S.A.	China	Mexico
1.5 liter bottle of water	$1.12	$0.19	$1.50	$0.56	$0.65
movie ticket	$11.75	$2.68	$10.50	$6.05	$3.15
meal in a restaurant	$15.30	$3.20	$13.00	$2.75	$5.10

2 **Read again and write.**

1 The most and least popular tourist destinations. ____France____ , _____ , _____

2 The most and least expensive countries to buy water. _____ , _____

3 The most and least popular vacation activities. _____ , _____

3 **Which country would you most like to visit and why?**

I'd love to go to China. There are beautiful places to visit there, and the food is amazing.

 **FIND OUT MORE**

How many tourists visit your country each year? What activities do they do?

Math: graphs and charts | learning to learn

1 **Read the blog post. What tourist attraction did Joshua visit? What activities did he enjoy?**

DID YOU KNOW...?
Niagara Falls, which is a waterfall between the U.S.A. and Canada, is the most visited tourist attraction in the world. It has about 30 million visitors every year!

A special vacation in Greece

Last summer my grandparents and I went to Greece on vacation, and I had the most amazing time. We stayed in the capital city, Athens, for three days, then we stayed on one of the islands.

Greece is a country in southern Europe that is famous for its ancient history and its beautiful islands. People live on 227 of the islands, but there are a lot more. The currency is the euro, and the official language is Greek. In the summer, the weather is hot and dry.

In Athens, we went sightseeing and visited a lot of ancient sites. For me, the most interesting place was the Parthenon, which is almost 2,500 years old! On the island, we went to the beach and went hiking in the mountains. Greek food is delicious, and the best thing I ate was moussaka, which is made of meat and vegetables.

It was the greatest vacation ever, and I really want to go back one day!

by Joshua

2 **Underline the superlatives in the blog post in Activity 1.**

3 **In pairs, discuss a place you have visited. Make notes in your notebook.**

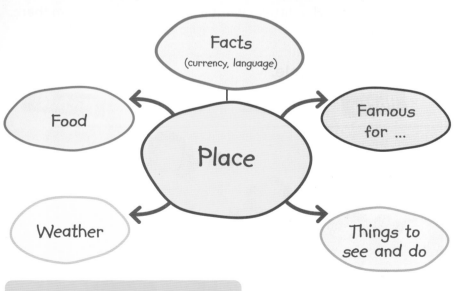

Learning to write:

Superlatives

We use superlatives to add interesting facts to our writing.

The most interesting place was the Parthenon.

Athens is **the biggest** city in Greece.

Ready to write:

Go to Workbook page 78.

Project

Research and plan a day trip to your place from Activity 3.

Math: graphs and charts | learning to learn 79

1 William is talking to his friend Sarah. What does Sarah say? Read the conversation and choose the best answer. Write a letter (A–H) for each answer.

William: Hi Sarah, how are you?
Sarah: ___B___

1 **William:** What are you writing in your notebook?
Sarah: _____

2 **William:** When are you going to Mexico?
Sarah: _____

3 **William:** What's the weather like in Mexico?
Sarah: _____

4 **William:** They speak Spanish in Mexico. Do you speak Spanish?
Sarah: _____

5 **William:** Have you been to Mexico before?
Sarah: _____
William: You're so lucky!

A Not yet. I went to Mexico last week.
B I'm fine, thanks.
C Never. This is the first time.
D Tomorrow afternoon. I need to get ready today.
E Very much. It's sunny most days.

F It's a list of all the things I need to take on vacation. I haven't packed my suitcase yet.
G It might be hot. So I'll have to take a lot of T-shirts and shorts.
H A little. I want to learn more when I'm there.

2 🎧 69 **Listen and draw lines. There is one example.**

Betty   David   Emma   Harry   Helen   Katy   Michael

3 Play the game. Ask and answer.

Around the world

Instructions: Throw a dice and move around the board. Make a sentence or ask your friend a question. If you make a mistake, you lose a turn.

Key

Green: Describe the picture.
Orange: *Have you ever … ?*
Yellow: *He's/She's just …*

> There are four purple plastic buttons.

> Have you ever won a prize?

> She's just drunk tea.

START

1 Read and choose "yes" or "no." Are you A, B, or C?

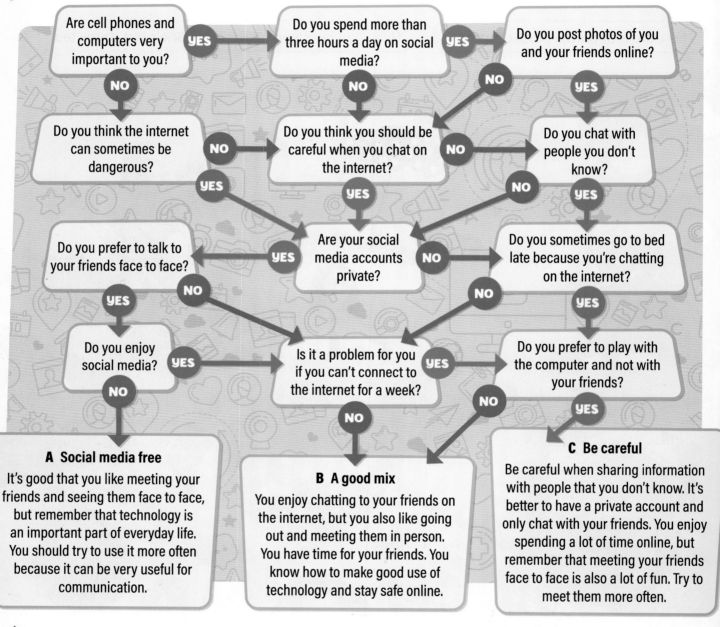

Are cell phones and computers very important to you? — **YES** → Do you spend more than three hours a day on social media? — **YES** → Do you post photos of you and your friends online?

Are cell phones and computers very important to you? — **NO** → Do you think the internet can sometimes be dangerous?

Do you spend more than three hours a day on social media? — **NO** → Do you think you should be careful when you chat on the internet?

Do you post photos of you and your friends online? — **NO** → Do you think you should be careful when you chat on the internet?

Do you post photos of you and your friends online? — **YES** → Do you chat with people you don't know?

Do you think the internet can sometimes be dangerous? — **NO** → Do you think you should be careful when you chat on the internet?

Do you think you should be careful when you chat on the internet? — **NO** → Do you chat with people you don't know?

Do you think the internet can sometimes be dangerous? — **YES** → Are your social media accounts private?

Do you think you should be careful when you chat on the internet? — **YES** → Are your social media accounts private?

Do you chat with people you don't know? — **NO** → Do you sometimes go to bed late because you're chatting on the internet?

Do you chat with people you don't know? — **YES** → Do you sometimes go to bed late because you're chatting on the internet?

Are your social media accounts private? — **YES** → Do you prefer to talk to your friends face to face?

Are your social media accounts private? — **NO** → Do you sometimes go to bed late because you're chatting on the internet?

Do you prefer to talk to your friends face to face? — **YES** → Do you enjoy social media?

Do you prefer to talk to your friends face to face? — **NO** → Is it a problem for you if you can't connect to the internet for a week?

Do you sometimes go to bed late because you're chatting on the internet? — **NO** → Is it a problem for you if you can't connect to the internet for a week?

Do you sometimes go to bed late because you're chatting on the internet? — **YES** → Do you prefer to play with the computer and not with your friends?

Do you enjoy social media? — **YES** → Is it a problem for you if you can't connect to the internet for a week?

Do you enjoy social media? — **NO** → **A**

Is it a problem for you if you can't connect to the internet for a week? — **YES** → Do you prefer to play with the computer and not with your friends?

Is it a problem for you if you can't connect to the internet for a week? — **NO** → **B**

Do you prefer to play with the computer and not with your friends? — **NO** → **B**

Do you prefer to play with the computer and not with your friends? — **YES** → **C**

A Social media free
It's good that you like meeting your friends and seeing them face to face, but remember that technology is an important part of everyday life. You should try to use it more often because it can be very useful for communication.

B A good mix
You enjoy chatting to your friends on the internet, but you also like going out and meeting them in person. You have time for your friends. You know how to make good use of technology and stay safe online.

C Be careful
Be careful when sharing information with people that you don't know. It's better to have a private account and only chat with your friends. You enjoy spending a lot of time online, but remember that meeting your friends face to face is also a lot of fun. Try to meet them more often.

2 Do you agree with your result? Talk to a partner. Ask and answer.

1 How many hours a day do you spend online?
2 Do you think three hours a day is too much or not enough?
3 How many hours a week do you spend with your friends face to face?
4 Do you ever go to bed late because you're chatting online?
5 Why can it be dangerous to chat with people that you don't know?

1 Look at the picture. What's wrong? What do you think is going to happen? Talk to a partner.

> Look at *f*. She isn't sitting safely.

> Yes, she's going to fall and hurt her back.

 2 Listen and check. Say the letter (a–h).

 3 How can you be safe at school? Write five sentences with "should" and "shouldn't."

> We shouldn't walk around the classroom with scissors.
> We should walk, not run, inside the school building.

Units 5&6 Values Helping at home

1 **Read and answer the questions.**

1 Why is Mr. Banks away from home so often?

2 How does the family work as a team?

3 What have Fred and Vicky learned?

http://www.davidsreports.com

David's reports

This week, I've been to visit the Banks family. They all help do jobs around the house and take care of Mrs. Banks.

David: Well, Mr. Banks, can you tell us about your family and how you all work together?

Mr. Banks: Yes, of course. My son Fred's 16, and my daughter Vicky's 13. We've worked hard as a family this year because my wife has been very sick.

David: Oh, I'm sorry. What do you mean when you say "worked hard"?

Mr. Banks: Well, during the year, I've been away from home often. I take my wife to the hospital, and I spend a lot of time there. So Fred and Vicky have learned to do a lot of things: they sometimes do the shopping, and when Fred cooks our meals, Vicky cleans the kitchen.

David: Not many children know how to cook and clean!

Mr. Banks: No. Fred saw the problem and asked me how he could help at home. We spent some Saturdays in

the kitchen, and I showed him how to make good meals. Now he's an excellent cook! Actually, he likes to choose the food himself, so he prefers to do the shopping.

David: That's great! And did you say that Vicky helps him in the kitchen?

Mr. Banks: That's right. She helps in a lot of other ways, too. Vicky cleans the house and washes the clothes.

David: Good job, Vicky! How do you feel about doing all these jobs?

Vicky: Well, actually, I don't see it as extra work now. It was difficult at first because I felt that I didn't have enough time to do these jobs, do my homework, and meet my friends. Now I've learned to do things better and more quickly, so I have a little more time. We all work as a team, and I feel good because I'm part of it. I'm very lucky to have a brother like Fred. He's been great.

David: That's a nice thing to hear your sister say. How do you feel about that, Fred?

Fred: Yes, it is a very nice thing to say, and I feel good, thanks. I think that before all this happened, I was a little lazy. I didn't do anything in the house, and my parents had to do everything. Now I'm really happy that I've learned to do a lot of things for myself and for others. I think we're both happy to help our parents. The most important thing for us is that Mom is feeling better now.

2 🎧 71 **Listen and say "Vicky," "Fred," or "Mr. Banks."**

3 **Talk to a partner about how you help at home.**

1 What do you do to help at home?

2 How can you help more at home?

Values: Units 5 & 6 *Helping at home* | social responsibilities

Units 7&8 Values Sharing problems

1 Read the posts and answer the questions.

REACH OUT – HELPLINE

Username: TheUnicorn | **Topic:** Online Bullying

Last week, I found my 11-year-old sister, Kim, crying in her bedroom. She told me that some other children at school have posted some terrible things about her online. She said this isn't the first time it's happened and that she's been worried about it for three weeks. She says the children who are doing it think it's funny and that it's only a joke, but she's very unhappy, and she doesn't want to go to school. She's asked me not to tell my parents. What should I do?

1 Why was Kim crying?
2 How long has she been worried?
3 Do you think it's funny?

REACH OUT – HELPLINE

Username: HeretoHelp | **Topic:** Online Bullying

This is very serious. Your sister is very unhappy. If she doesn't want to go to school, she needs help right now. This situation has lasted long enough, and it might get worse. You've listened to your sister, and that has helped her, but she really needs the advice of a grown-up. You have to tell your parents. It might be a good idea for them to speak to your sister's teachers. We can understand that you may feel that you shouldn't tell your parents the secret, but it's really the best way to help your sister.

4 What does Kim need?
5 What does TheUnicorn have to do?

REACH OUT – HELPLINE

Username: RockStar

Topic: Unfriendly Friends

An old friend has moved into the house next to mine. We've been friends since we were three, but she's a girl and I'm a boy. She's very funny and she makes me laugh, but my friends on the basketball team have started to laugh at me because I'm friends with a girl. They call me terrible names, and they've blocked me on our social media group so that I can't chat with them. I feel very angry and unhappy, but I don't want to lose any of my friends. Please help me. What should I do?

6 What's the problem with RockStar's old friend?
7 Why does he feel angry and unhappy?

2 Talk to a partner about RockStar's post. Imagine that you are HeretoHelp.

1 Who can RockStar talk to?
2 What should he do?

3 Write a reply to RockStar's post. Use the words in the box.

might   should / shouldn't
need to   has to / doesn't have to

Grammar reference

1 Going to
We use *going to* to talk about plans.

Affirmative	Negative	Question
I'm going to ride a bike.	I'm not going to ride a bike.	Am I going to ride a bike?
She's going to ride a bike.	She isn't going to ride a bike.	Is she going to ride a bike?
They're going to ride a bike.	They aren't going to ride a bike.	Are they going to ride a bike?

2 Will
We use *will* to talk about predictions for the future.

Affirmative	Negative	Question
It'll travel to the moon.	It won't travel to the moon.	Will it travel to the moon?
We'll travel to the moon.	We won't travel to the moon.	Will we travel to the moon?

3 Past progressive
We use the past progressive to describe what was happening in the past.

Affirmative	Negative	Question
I was working when you arrived.	I wasn't working when you arrived.	Was I working when you arrived?
He was working when you arrived.	He wasn't working when you arrived.	Was he working when you arrived?
They were working when you arrived.	They weren't working when you arrived.	Were they working when you arrived?

4 Countable and uncountable nouns

Countable nouns	Uncountable nouns
We can count them: apples, bananas, carrots	We can't count them: bread, sugar, water
How many bananas are there?	How much water is there?
There are too many bananas.	There's too much water.
There aren't many bananas.	There isn't much water.
There aren't enough bananas.	There isn't enough water.

Present perfect and adverbs

I still haven't done my homework. (= But I have to do it soon.)
She's been sick since Monday. (= When? A point in time: time, date, day, etc.)
They've been sick for two days. (= How long? How many minutes, hours, days, weeks, etc.)
Have you ever had a fish for a pet? (= At any time in your life)
I've never seen a dolphin. (= At no time in my life)

Pronouns

some	any	no	every
someone	anyone	no one	everyone
something	anything	nothing	everything
somewhere	anywhere	nowhere	everywhere

There's someone at the door.	There isn't anyone at the door. Is there anyone at the door?	There's no one at the door.	Everyone's at the door.
I have something to tell you.	I don't have anything to tell you. Do you have anything to tell me?	I have nothing to tell you.	I'm going to tell you everything.
They're going somewhere.	They aren't going anywhere. Are they going anywhere?	They're going nowhere.	They're going everywhere.

Possibility

I may buy the skirt.
It might rain.
I may not buy the skirt.
It might not rain.

Present perfect and adverbs

You've just sent the email.	You haven't sent the email yet.	Have you sent the email yet?
She's already sent the email.	She hasn't sent the email yet.	Has she sent the email yet?

Flyers Listening

1 🎧 **72** **Listen and complete the information. Then check with a partner.**

How do you spell that?

First name: _____Holly_____

1 Last name: _____

2 School: _____

3 Date of birth: October 26th, _____

4 Library password: _____

5 I want to join because:

interested in _____

books can help with _____

2 🎧 **73** 🐵 **Listen and write. There is one example.**

A new adventure

Place opens for the first time:
on September _____3rd_____

1 Visit to: _____ Castle

2 Age: _____ years old

3 Travel from town: by _____

4 Views of: _____

5 People like: the _____

Flyers Listening

1 🎧 74 **Listen. Write who the objects belong to. Use the box to help you. Then listen again and color.**

Betty   Grace   ~~Oliver~~   Peter   Robert

Lost Property Office

Oliver

2 🎧 75 🐵 **What did family and friends give George for his trip? Listen and write a letter in each box. There is one example.**

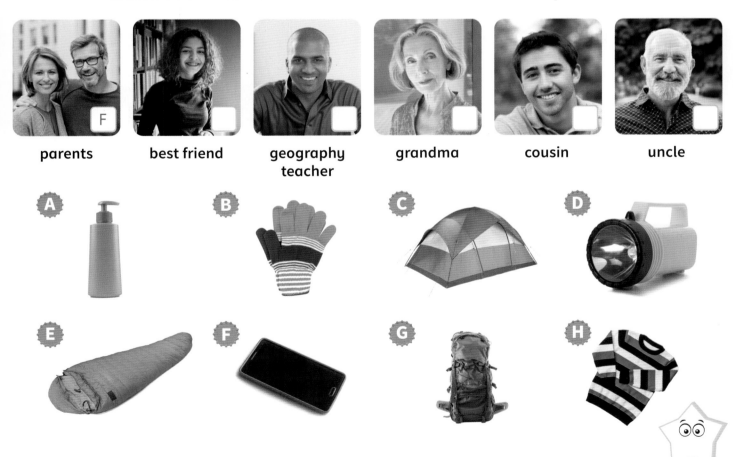

parents   best friend   geography teacher   grandma   cousin   uncle

Flyers Reading and Writing

1 📝 **Read the sentences and choose the best answer. Draw lines and match. Then complete each answer in your notebook.**

1 Should we have a picnic in the park tomorrow afternoon?

2 The school bus might not come today because it's snowing!

3 Why is your grandma laughing?

4 What time will the train come?

5 Should I buy George a drum for his birthday?

6 Are you going to the concert tomorrow night?

A Oh, she's happy because …

B I think it arrives at …

C Good idea! I'll bring some popcorn and …

D No, he doesn't like …

E Yes, I'm really excited! It starts at …

F Oh, no! We're going to be …

2 🐵 **It's Monday afternoon. Richard is talking to Sophia about her birthday on Saturday. What does Sophia say? Read the conversation and choose the best answer. Write a letter (A–H) for each answer. You do not need to use all the letters. There is one example.**

Example

Richard: Hi, Sophia. What did you do for your birthday on Saturday?

Sophia: _____ G _____

Questions

1 **Richard:** Where did you go?

Sophia: _____

2 **Richard:** Is that the one on the top floor of that new skyscraper?

Sophia: _____

3 **Richard:** Was the food good?

Sophia: _____

4 **Richard:** I hope you had a birthday cake!

Sophia: _____

5 **Richard:** Did you also go to the festival in the park that night?

Sophia: _____

A We went there after the meal. The music was great.

B Of course! We all enjoyed a piece at home earlier.

C It was a new place called High Five.

D They're my favorite band.

E Yes! I ate a vegetable dish I'd never tried before.

F It wasn't easy eating with chopsticks.

G My parents took me and some friends out to eat.

H Yes, the views were amazing!

Flyers Reading and Writing

1 Read and write the correct word.

1 Elephants **is** amazing animals.
       _____are_____

2 Eating fruit and vegetables **no** day is healthy.
      _____

3 Skyscrapers are taller **that** trees.
      _____

4 Ponds are places **who** you find frogs.
      _____

5 One day, people will **living** on the moon.
      _____

6 In the past, people **make** fires to cook on.
      _____

2 Read the text. Choose the right words and write them on the lines.

	The tent
Example	People _____have_____ used tents in different environments for thousands of years.
1	In the past, people lived in _____ because they didn't
2	have houses like we do today. People _____ stay in one place for very long. They took their animals to better places to feed in spring or winter and often walked
3	hundreds of kilometers _____ sell and buy food or important objects. Tents were heavy to carry but easy to make from trees and animal fur. They helped people feel safer at night.
4	_____, donkeys and camels carried explorers' tents on their long journeys
5	_____ jungles and across deserts to new countries. Tents also kept maps and diaries dry and safe.
6	Today _____ is a popular activity for many families and friends on weekends
7	and during vacations. People enjoy _____ outside in a tent and being in the
8	country, _____ from noisy, busy cities.
9	Tents are still usually the same shape _____ in the past, but they are now made of lighter materials. Many people who love hiking a lot on vacation can carry them
10	in or under their backpacks. They are also easier to put up _____.

Example	did	can	(have)			
1	it	them	their	6	camp	camping	camped
2	don't	haven't	didn't	7	sleep	slept	sleeping
3	to	for	by	8	away	instead	over
4	Early	Finally	Later	9	with	to	as
5	until	through	during	10	quick	quickly	quickest

Flyers Reading and Writing

1 Cross out the word that doesn't belong.

1 have … **time / fun / ~~hungry~~ / a headache**

2 go to … **bed / asleep / a hospital / school**

3 make … **friends / a cake / a noise / the doctor's office**

4 be … **Spain / careful / tired / late**

5 take … **medicine / east / a test / a bus**

6 feel … **well / cold / online / excited**

2 Read the diary and write the missing words. Write one word on each line.

Example	My dad _____has_____ just started a new job, and we've moved to a new city. I really love our new
1	apartment. It's on the 20th _____, so the views are amazing.
2	Right now, my parents _____ driving me to my new school.
3	I _____ them I was feeling worried about my first day.
4	Then Mom showed me there were four science classes a week in the schedule. That made me happy _____ it's my favorite subject!
5	There will _____ a school skiing trip this winter, which sounds exciting, too.
	I just hope my classmates are friendly!

Flyers Reading and Writing

1 📝 **Look and write four or five words under each picture. Discuss your ideas with a partner. Then write a sentence for each picture in your notebook.**

_____   _____   _____

_____   _____   _____

_____   _____   _____

2 📝🐵 **Look at the three pictures. Write about this story. Write 20 or more words.**

_____

_____

_____

Flyers Speaking

1 Look and circle the words. Number the pictures in order.
Tell the story with a partner.

A scary cave

bicycle   animal   river   backpack

blanket   cave   castle   rock

woods   gate

desert   flashlight

entrance   pocket

fire   sandwich

beetle   bat

2 These pictures tell a story. It's called "Lucky Teddy."
Just look at the pictures first. Now you tell the story.

Lucky Teddy!

> Holly and her brother, David, are walking down a path next to a river with their mom and their dog. David wants to look at the waterfall.

David

Holly

Flyers Speaking

1 Read the instructions. Play the game. Interview a partner.

Instructions: Roll the dice only once for each turn.
Go to the correct section of the game.
Answer your partner's questions.
Use the color key to color the *Tell me* square.
The winner is the first to answer all the questions and color all the *Tell me* squares.

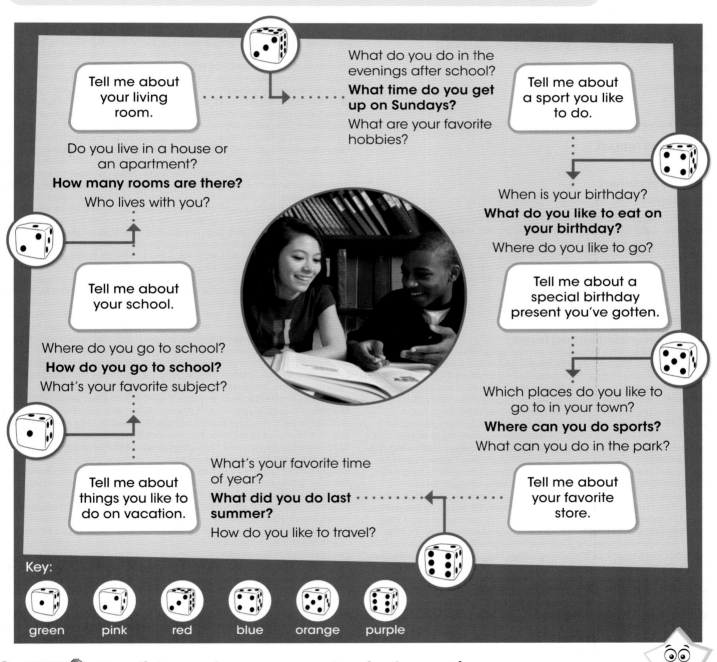

Tell me about your living room.

What do you do in the evenings after school?
What time do you get up on Sundays?
What are your favorite hobbies?

Tell me about a sport you like to do.

Do you live in a house or an apartment?
How many rooms are there?
Who lives with you?

When is your birthday?
What do you like to eat on your birthday?
Where do you like to go?

Tell me about your school.

Tell me about a special birthday present you've gotten.

Where do you go to school?
How do you go to school?
What's your favorite subject?

Which places do you like to go to in your town?
Where can you do sports?
What can you do in the park?

What's your favorite time of year?
What did you do last summer?
How do you like to travel?

Tell me about things you like to do on vacation.

Tell me about your favorite store.

Key:

green   pink   red   blue   orange   purple

2 🎧 76 Now listen and answer your teacher's questions.

Thanks and Acknowledgments

Authors' thanks

Many thanks to everyone at Cambridge University Press & Assessment for their dedication and hard work, and in particular to:

Louise Wood for doing such a great job overseeing the level; Liz Wilkie for her hard work and great editorial assistance; freelance editors Melissa Bryant and Stephanie Howard.

We would also like to thank all our students and colleagues, past, present, and future, at Star English academy in Murcia, especially Jim Kelly for his friendship and support throughout the years.

Dedications

To Alison Sharpe for seeing the potential, to Maria Pylas for driving it forward, to Susan Gonzalez for believing in and championing it, and to Liane Grainger for keeping us excellent, steadfast company throughout the whole of our stellar journey. – CN and MT

Illustration

Ana Sebastian (Bright Agency); Dave Williams (Bright Agency); David Belmont (Beehive); Javier Joaquin (Beehive); Laszlo Veres (Beehive); Moreno Chiacchiera (Beehive); Shahab (Sylvie Poggio Artists).

Audio

Audio production by John Marshall Media.

Video

Video acknowledgments are in the Teacher Resources on Cambridge One.

Design and typeset

Blooberry Design

Additional authors

Rebecca Legros (CLIL); Montse Watkin (Sounds and life skills, Exam folder)

The authors and publishers acknowledge the following sources of copyright material and are grateful for the permissions granted. While every effort has been made, it has not always been possible to identify the sources of all the material used, or to trace all copyright holders. If any omissions are brought to our notice, we will be happy to include the appropriate acknowledgments on reprinting and in the next update to the digital edition, as applicable.

Key: U = Unit, R = Review, V = Values, EF = Exam folder

Photography

All photos are sourced from Getty Images.

U0: daboost/iStock/Getty Images Plus; Anastassiya Bezhekeneva/Moment; T3 Magazine/Future; JGI/Tom Grill/Tetra images; Daviles/iStock/Getty Images Plus; Lane Oatey/Blue Jean Images; kate_sept2004/E+; PonyWang/E+; Roman Bykhalets/iStock/Getty Images Plus; Lesia_G/iStock/Getty Images Plus; watchara_tongnoi/iStock/Getty Images Plus; Sergio Delle Vedove/EyeEm; SMSka/iStock/Getty Images Plus; Ilyabolotov/iStock/Getty Images Plus; U1: Klaus Vedfelt/DigitalVision; Neurobite/iStock/Getty Images Plus; MistikaS/E+; Keren Su/Photodisc; Helmut Meyer zur Capellen/imageBROKER; PHAS/Universal Images Group; DEA/A. DE GREGORIO/De Agostini; Dallas and John Heaton/The Image Bank Unreleased; Will \u0026 Deni McIntyre/Corbis Documentary; Image Source/DigitalVision; Thomas Barwick/DigitalVision; Peter Dazeley/The Image Bank; TPopova/iStock/Getty Images Plus; fcw5/iStock/Getty Images Plus; General Photographic Agency/Hulton Archive; stevenallan/iStock Unreleased; mattjeacock/iStock Unreleased; ly86/DigitalVision Vectors; Lidiia Moor/iStock/Getty Images Plus; Naddiya/iStock/Getty Images Plus; invincible_bulldog/iStock/Getty Images Plus; Elen11/iStock/Getty Images Plus; MsMoloko/iStock/Getty Images Plus; seamartini/iStock/Getty Images Plus U2: Hector Roqueta Rivero/Moment; IlexImage/E+; artisteer/iStock/Getty Images Plus; RedBarnStudio/E+; Serjio74/iStock/Getty Images Plus; Vladimiroquai/iStock/Getty Images Plus; Stockbyte; Jonathan Knowles/Stone; dima_zel/iStock/Getty Images Plus; Frank Rossoto Stocktrek/DigitalVision; RichVintage/E+; FatCamera/E+; dima_zel/iStock/Getty Images Plus; Stocktrek Images; Bloomberg Creative/Bloomberg Creative Photos; skynesher/E+; gorodenkoff/iStock/Getty Images Plus; Jonathan Kitchen/DigitalVision; Nitat Termmee/Moment; Digital Art/The Image Bank; Mlenny/E+; egal/iStock/Getty Images Plus; Westend61; U3: Nastasic/DigitalVision Vectors; Dea Picture Library/De Agostini; Kurt Desplenter/AFP; Felix Cesare/Moment; Alexander Blotnitsky/AFP; Paul Souders/DigitalVision; evemilla/E+; Ryan McVay/Photodisc; herreid/iStock/Getty Images Plus; Engdao Wichitpunya/EyeEm; 4x6/E+; FangXiaNuo/E+; Christoph Wagner/Moment; VectorMine/iStock/Getty Images Plus; gniedzieska/iStock/Getty Images Plus; Â© Marco Bottigelli/Moment; Andre Schoenherr/Stone; Mark Garlick/Science Photo Library; -/AFP; katatonia82/iStock/Getty Images Plus; vitalik19111992/iStock/Getty Images Plus; U4: Aleksandr Zubkov/Moment; Burcu Atalay Tankut/Moment; FatManPhotoUK/iStock/Getty Images Plus; udra/iStock/Getty Images Plus; pilipphoto/iStock/Getty Images Plus; Roberto Machado Noa/Moment; Nirad/iStock/Getty Images Plus; Image Source; Natalya Trofimchuk/iStock/Getty Images Plus; fcafotodigital/E+; Carlo A/Moment; Milena_Vuckovic/iStock/Getty Images Plus; GMVozd/E+; Westend61; jointstar/iStock/Getty Images Plus; VvoeVale/iStock/Getty Images Plus; nehopelon/iStock/Getty Images Plus; The Washington Post; MaskaRad/iStock/Getty Images Plus; Anna Reinert/imageBroker; alvarez/E+; Steve Cicero/Photodisc; olgakr/iStock/Getty Images Plus; SiberianArt/iStock/Getty Images Plus; akkachai thothubthai/iStock/Getty Images Plus; sangidan idan/iStock/Getty Images Plus; U5: Ana Guisado Photography/Moment; Mike Hill/Stone; Catherine Falls Commercial/Moment; Hugh Threlfall/Moment Mobile; Gabriele Grassl/iStock/Getty Images Plus; nomadimagesuk/iStock/Getty Images Plus; Westend61; Robbie Goodall/Moment; C'est les photos que j'aime…/Moment; SolStock/E+; LeManna/iStock/Getty Images Plus; Burazin/The Image Bank; Andrea Gambadoro – Filmmaker and Photographer/Moment; Oleksandr Vakulin/EyeEm; Nattapong Leardprasit/EyeEm; George Karbus Photography/Image Source; Raimundo Fernandez Diez/Moment; Hal Beral/Corbis; by wildestanimal/Moment; Portra/DigitalVision; Ron Levine/DigitalVision; tetmc/iStock/Getty Images Plus; Tom Werner/DigitalVision; Jose Luis Pelaez Inc/DigitalVision; Humberto Ramirez/Moment; Andrew Peacock/Stone; VivianG/iStock/Getty Images Plus; Gabrielle Yap/EyeEm; Reinhard Dirscherl/The Image Bank; Ippei Naoi/Moment; Rajni Singh/EyeEm; Photo taken by Kami (Kuo, Jia-Wei)/Moment; alexander uhrin/iStock/Getty Images Plus; Vijay Talla/EyeEm; Silvia Otte/Stone; Puripatl/iStock/Getty Images Plus; Jeff J Mitchell/Getty Images News; eugenesergeev/iStock/Getty Images Plus; MrJub/iStock/Getty Images Plus; FoxysGraphic/iStock/Getty Images Plus; LuisAlvarez/Digital Vision U6: Purdue9394/E+; mediaphotos/iStock/Getty Images Plus; CasarsaGuru/E+; Robert Niedring/Cavan; Tgordievskaya/iStock/Getty Images Plus; Jupiterimages/Goodshoot; Westend61; Joe McBride/The Image Bank; lovro77/E+; FamVeld/iStock/Getty Images Plus; shironosov/iStock/Getty Images Plus; Seamind Panadda/EyeEm; brebca/iStock/Getty Images Plus; Wirote Banhachai/EyeEm; artproem/iStock/Getty Images Plus; DougLemke/iStock/Getty Images Plus; Aneese/iStock/Getty Images Plus; soopareuk/iStock/Getty Images Plus; Nikada/iStock Unreleased; Monty Rakusen/Image Source; DigitalVision; FoxysGraphic/iStock/Getty Images Plus; prospero_design/E+ U7: Yobro10/iStock/Getty Images Plus; Antonio_Diaz/iStock/Getty Images Plus; Brian Mitchell/Corbis Documentary; damircudic/E+; Mario Marco/Moment; Weerayut Ranmai/EyeEm; Ng Sok Lian/EyeEm; Kwanchai Lerttanapunyaporn/EyeEm; MirageC/Moment; Alicia Llop/Moment; Image Source; Mali Li Lxm/EyeEm; Last Resort/Photodisc; popovaphoto/iStock/Getty Images Plus; Prasert Krainukul/Moment; olegbreslavtsev/iStock/Getty Images Plus; pearleye/E+; Andrei Naumenka/iStock/Getty Images Plus; SEAN GLADWELL/Moment; bubaone/DigitalVision Vectors; Maydaymayday/DigitalVision Vectors; smartboy10/DigitalVision Vectors; U8: SDI Productions/E+; kali9/E+; ferrantraite/E+; Pongasn68/iStock/Getty Images Plus; Razvan/iStock Editorial; Mekdet/Moment; lukyeee1976/iStock/Getty Images Plus; luchschen/iStock/Getty Images Plus; janrysavy/E+; Imgorthand/E+; Tom Werner/DigitalVision; monkeybusinessimages/iStock/Getty Images Plus; Paul Wigfield/EyeEm; Richmatts/E+; SHansche/iStock/Getty Images Plus; isil terzioglu/iStock/Getty Images Plus; Mark Astakhov/iStock/Getty Images Plus; AndyRoland/iStock/Getty Images Plus; Imgorthand/E+; Ennessy/iStock/Getty Images Plus; R12: Hector Roqueta Rivero/Moment; R26: narvikk/E+; R44: kali9/E+; R62: Jon Hicks/Stone; Jupiterimages/Photos.com\u003e; FG Trade/E+; Tetra Images; Yellow Dog Productions/The Image Bank; Marc Dufresne/E+; monkeybusinessimages/iStock/Getty Images Plus; Ariel Skelley/DigitalVision; R80: FG Trade/E+; Stocktrek Images; ratmaner/iStock/Getty Images Plus; Shedu/iStock/Getty Images Plus; ttatty/iStock/Getty Images Plus; Sebastian Ramirez Morales/Moment; leitmotif425/iStock/Getty Images Plus; 3djewelry/iStock/Getty Images Plus; wanderluster/E+; Carlos Salsamendi/EyeEm; blackCAT/E+; AleksandarNakic/E+; Ekaterina Pereslavtseva/EyeEm; Barry Austin/DigitalVision; Chris Tobin/DigitalVision; Noel Hendrickson/DigitalVision; Jamie Grill/Tetra images; Westend61; Sam Edwards/OJO Images; Jaakko Paarvala/Moment; Alistair Berg/DigitalVision; Caia Image/Collection Mix: Subjects; V82: ConceptCafe/iStock/Getty Images Plus; Picnote/iStockphoto/Getty Images; V84: JGI/Tom Grill/Tetra images; MoMo Productions/DigitalVision; V85: lushik/DigitalVision Vectors; Anna Erastova/iStock/Getty Images Plus; EF: Johner Images/Johner Images Royalty-Free; Westend61; Oliver Rossi/DigitalVision; David A Land/Tetra images; Tom Merton/OJO Images; eurobanks/iStock/Getty Images Plus; Tim Robberts/DigitalVision; vav63/iStock/Getty Images Plus; Amphawan Chanunpha/iStock/Getty Images Plus; benimage/E+; skodonnell/E+; lucentius/E+; phwphr bdinthr phathr/EyeEm; valio84sl/iStock/Getty Images Plus; barisonal/E+; Ganesh Bastola/Moment; Maskot; Inti St Clair/DigitalVision.

Cover photography by Tiffany Mumford for Creative Listening

Commissioned photography by Stephen Noble and Duncan Yeldham for Creative Listening